More Than Wanderers

More Than Wanderers

SPIRITUAL DISCIPLINES FOR
CHRISTIAN MINISTRY

James C. Fenhagen

A Crossroad Book

THE SEABURY PRESS · NEW YORK

1978
The Seabury Press
815 Second Avenue
New York, N.Y. 10017

Printed in the United States of America

Library of Congress Cataloging in Publication Data
Fenhagen, James C   More than wanderers.
"A Crossroad book."
1. Meditation.   2. Christian life—Anglican
authors.   I. Title.
BV4813.F45   248'.48'3   77-17974   ISBN 0-8164-0386-4

For
Henri Nouwen,
Anthony Gerald, OHC,
Elizabeth O'Connor,
and
the All Saints Sisters of the Poor

who, knowingly and unknowingly,
have been for me
companions along the way

Contents

Introduction

Whoever offers me the sacrifice of
thanksgiving honors me;
But to those who keep in my way will
I show the salvation of God.

The underlying motif of this book can best be expressed in these words from the last verse of the fif-
tieth Psalm.

This book is written for those within the Christian
tradition who are trying to establish workable patterns
that will enable them to walk more firmly "in the
way." It is offered, therefore, as a guide for establishing an inner discipline that is at the same time both
worldly and contemplative. Its approach is un-
apologetically Christian, yet is open to all that is to be
learned from the other great religious traditions of the
world, as well as from the creative insights emerging
from humanistic studies within the secular disciplines.
Many Christians in the Church today are deeply serious about their spiritual journeys, yet are put off by
undue piety and religious sentimentality. They are
seeking an inner discipline which affirms that living is
as much struggle as it is celebration, a spirituality

which takes seriously both the need for continuous critical exploration and a deepened responsibility for the world in which we live. This book seeks to honor these concerns.

Several years ago I had a long conversation with a friend who had spent many years developing a program which sought to train and support laity in ministry within the settings where they were employed. After some very creative years, the program came to an end. In reflecting on the experience my friend made this comment: "The program lacked sustaining power because we didn't take seriously the need for developing the kind of inner discipline that would enable persons to be sustained by the power of God working from within. We worked hard at the 'outer journey' and were effective, but without the kind of inner life that will stand up under the pressures of the world, we soon lost our staying power." I have remembered these words for a long time. During the sixties the Church learned a lot about what it means to be involved in the struggle for liberation and peace. These were learnings that will be forgotten at our peril, especially at a time when so many people are beginning to test out the paths to inward awareness. It is of critical importance that we learn what it means to drink from the "inner spring," not as an escape from the hard realities of life, but rather as the way which, in Christ, we seek to engage these hard realities. Our task is to rediscover at every level of our being what it means to live "in Christ."

The aim of this book, therefore, is to link together in practice the worlds of meditation and ministry for, in the deepest sense, these worlds are one and the same. Christian prayer by its very nature expresses itself in ministry. Christian ministry is empowered and focused in prayer. Both begin and end in an ever-deepening awareness of Jesus Christ. The book, therefore, begins with the encounter with Christ, moves on to examine the nature of the ministry which results from that encounter and then seeks to develop an approach to prayer by which this ministry can be sustained. The remainder of the book builds on these theological underpinnings, paying particular attention to the actual practice of meditative prayer, the keeping of a journal and the use of a spiritual guide. The last chapter suggests ways in which the local church might incorporate some of these thoughts within its ongoing program.

The particular approach to Christian spirituality developed in this book has emerged out of my own struggle to grasp the deeper dimensions of my profession of faith. My own journey has been made up of periods of deep intensity and deep resistance, at times leveling off into a smooth flow when life seemed together and full, only to be interrupted by unplanned for events from without or unexpected movement from within that served to throw me off course. I have been deeply influenced by the insights of the human potential movement and depth psychology. I have worked with the disciplines of Zen and Yoga and have found in these ancient disciplines fresh avenues which have allowed me to pass through the blocks that have cut me off from my own tradition. In all of this, however, I have discovered a remarkable fact. The more I have worked at the discipline of regular meditation, the more intense has been my yearning for my own tradition. The deeper my journey into my inner life, the more profound has become my thirst for a living experience of the Man from Nazareth.

Unlike Transcendental Meditation, Zen or the way of the Sufis, Christian meditation focuses sharply on the Person of Jesus Christ. It is in Him that we are led to behold the mystery of the Father. The purpose of Christian meditation is to become "Christ-conscious"—to live more deeply in Him, that He might live through us. The methods and suggestions offered in this book are intended to assist in making Christ-consciousness more truly a reality for the Christian seeker.

For the past four years, as part of the Church and Ministry Program of the Hartford Seminary Foundation, I have taught courses in Christian spirituality to groups of clergy and laity at centers throughout New England and in numerous parish churches. My own journey has been deeply influenced by this experience. What follows in these pages has been shaped by loving encounter with people who, like myself, possess no special insight into the mystery of faith, but who, by the Grace of God, have chosen to take their life journeys seriously. In my book, *Mutual Ministry*, I attempted to describe what this might involve. I wrote that, "One of the most critical tasks of the local church is to enable people to become 'journeyers' rather than 'wanderers.' "[1] This book is an outgrowth of that thought. It is written for those who, in their own way, choose to be *more than wanderers*.

No book is written alone. I am still indebted to those who have written books that have provided me with new thoughts and stimulated me to work harder at shaping those thoughts of my own that were still unformed. I am indebted to those persons who have been with me in classes and workshops and have reacted to what I have had to say, and who have shared with me the fruit of their own experiences. Finally, I am immensely grateful to my friends Earl Brill of the College of Preachers in Washington, D.C., and Victor Ross of Glastonbury, Connecticut for their assistance. I am also grateful for the support and encouragement of those at the Hartford Seminary Foundation with whom I work, especially Amy Beveridge and Audrey Ermakovich who have typed and retyped these pages, offering valuable suggestions along the way. Together we offer this book as an expression of our common ministry.

More Than Wanderers

CHAPTER I

A Theology
for the Christian Journey

Lord, you have searched me out and known me;
you know my sitting down and my rising up;
you discern my thoughts from afar.

You trace my journeys and my resting-places
and are acquainted with all my ways.

PSALM 139 VS. 1 and 2.

A God-seeker is a person on a journey. When the thirst has been awakened, we are no longer persons wandering aimlessly about, but rather persons who have begun to discern the bare outlines of a path. We become more than wanderers. We are people seeking for those signs that will point us in the direction that will allow our journey to unfold. For those whose thirst has led them into an encounter with Jesus of Nazareth, the signs that mark the way are grounded in an ancient and consistent tradition.

The Christian journey is indissolubly linked with a person. It is not a journey that we take alone. "Since Jesus was delivered to you as Christ and Lord," wrote St. Paul to that fledgling community of Christians

I

gathered in the city of Colossae, "live your lives in union with him. Be rooted in him, be built in him, be consolidated in the faith you were taught; let your hearts overflow with thankfulness" (Colossians 2:6–8).

Paul's words are not so much an injunction as they are a description of a relationship—a relationship already initiated by God's act. At the very moment we discover within ourselves the urge to respond to those deep yearnings that are so hard to put into words, we discover that God has already begun. We discover to our surprise that we have not chosen Him, but rather He has chosen us. In this recognition the journey in faith begins.

The Scriptures are full of stories about new beginnings. "The time has come," Jesus told the crowds as he made his way through Galilee. "The kingdom of God is upon you; repent and believe the Gospel" (Mark 1:15). This is where it all starts. We come to that point in our lives when we are ready to make a turn—to put behind us all those things that have bent our lives out of shape—and to enter into a new kind of relationship based on the belief that Jesus Christ is as present to us today as he was in the first century.

The Christian faith is a story of new beginnings. It is a story of repentance and forgiveness, of life emerging out of the experience of death. It is a journey which begins with the recognition that there is more to life than meets the eye—that without the healing and sustaining power of God our lives are incomplete. It is a journey which begins with the incredible fact of our unconditional acceptance by God. There is nothing we can do to earn or prove our worth. Our worth has been affirmed once and for all by the offering of Jesus Christ on our behalf. The Christian journey begins when, as forgiven and affirmed people, we ever so tentatively risk letting our lives be shaped and empowered by the Person of Jesus Christ. As the Gospel proclaims, because He lives, we live also with new possibility and purpose. Instead of being "takers," we become "givers," members of a community struggling to live in the world in a new way.

A PEOPLE WITH A MINISTRY

When we talk about the Christian journey or the disciplines of the Spirit, therefore, we do so in a particular context. God is actively at work in His world. He seeks to liberate the world from that seemingly endless grip of violence and injustice that we human beings perpetrate upon each other. Jesus Christ is the focal point of this liberation. In His cross and resurrection, He broke the power of those fears and drives that distort who we are and what we were meant to be. "God was in Christ," we proclaim, "reconciling the world to Himself" (II Corinthians 5:19).

The Christian journeyer is part of a worshipping community that believes this to be true. We are part of a community of people who in obedience to Jesus Christ are called to celebrate and participate in what God is doing in the world. The Christian Church is not

primarily an idea, a place or a building, but a people involved in a worldwide historical movement of cosmic
dimensions. As will be affirmed over and over again in
these pages, we are a people who have been given a
"ministry," a word that describes those things we do
as participants in the liberating activity of God: loving,
caring, healing, proclaiming, releasing.

The Christian journey is rooted in a particular context. Its aim is not personal fulfillment (although this
might well occur), nor the ecstasy of the experience of
God (although this might occur as well). Its aim is to
make it possible at ever-deepening levels for us to
share in Christ's ministry to the world. It is for this
that we need once again to learn to pray as a community. It is for this that the disciplines of prayer not only
make sense, but take on a note of urgency.

In her book, *The New Community*, Elizabeth
O'Connor tells the story of a remarkable encounter
between Thomas Merton and the Dalai Lama, the
spiritual leader of the Tibetan Buddhists. As a Trappist
monk, Merton led the way in establishing dialogue between monks of the Christian tradition and those of the
Buddhist East. On this particular occasion, Merton
was confronted by the Dalai Lama with a probing
question: "What do your vows oblige you to do? Do
they simply constitute an agreement to stick around
for life in the monastery? Or do they imply a commitment to a life of progress up certain mystical stages?"

After much hesitation, Merton stated what he understood his vows to be about. "I believe they can be

interpreted as a commitment to a total inner transformation of one sort or another, a commitment to become a completely new man. No matter where one attempts to do this, that remains the essential thing.'' Reflecting on these words, Elizabeth O'Connor, out of her very different tradition makes this comment: ''I also come to Merton's understanding. The vows that we make when we become members of the Church of Jesus Christ are more than an oath to stick around with a particular group of people. I believe that they can be interpreted as a commitment to a total inner transformation. . . . The transformation which takes place as we try to live out our lives with those who are also called to be on the same inward path is simply learning to live by love—learning to be persons in community with other persons. This is the most creative and difficult work to which any of us will ever be called. There is no higher achievement in all the world than to be a person in community, and this is the call of every Christian. We are to be builders of liberating communities that free love in us and free love in others.''[1]

Elizabeth O'Connor's words stand as magnificent witness to the meaning of Christian ministry. Any discussion of Christian ministry or the inner journey must ultimately come to terms with the issue she raises. At its most personal level, the Christian faith is concerned with nothing less than inner transformation. We are called to a life that seeks to reflect at ever-deepening levels the quality and character of the life of Christ himself. "I have been crucified with Christ," writes St. Paul. "The life I now live is not my life, but the life which Christ lives in me" (Galatians 2:20). This is the aim of our pilgrimage—to be transformed in such a way that the Lord might make Himself known through us.

When we ponder the implications of what it means to be transformed from within, it is indeed an awesome thought. No wonder there is resistance deep within us. No wonder we so often veer off or back away. We are being asked to experience the world in a new way, to see life through the eyes of another, with the promise that in so doing, we will discover the secret of life itself.

THE STRUGGLE WITH ONESELF

Transformation is born out of the struggle to come to terms with oneself. It is deepened by continuous encounter with the biblical story. It is sustained by a life lived in the community of faith. "Let your minds be remade and your whole nature thus transformed," pleads St. Paul (Romans 12:2). Only by the working of the Spirit within us can the living image of Christ be formed. Transformation is therefore a process that bears further examination.

Inner transformation is the work of God, but it is intimately connected with our growth toward wholeness. In my own life, while I have known a great deal of joy, I have also known pain. As I reflect on how my journey has unfolded, it is very clear that change has come about for me as a direct result of those occasions when, by the grace of God, I have been able to face pain, to struggle with the dark side of my life which I find so hard to own.

The biblical story of Jacob wrestling with God points to this dimension of the transformation process. Left alone, Jacob was forced to wrestle with God. He prevailed and received God's blessing, but walked away limping. As we struggle with the dark and un-known part of ourselves—the hurts, the fears, the un-answered questions and the unresolved struggles—we wrestle with God. In this profound and mysterious en-counter the process of inner transformation seems to find its root. Robert Raines has managed to capture something of this mystery. He writes:

Jacob was named and lamed. You and I will be given a new name, a new identity, if we struggle to the dawn-death, and a scar to remember it by. No naming without a laming. God scars those he names with some mark of meaning, some thorn in the flesh which we bear in our bodies all our days to remind us we have seen God face to face.[2]

Loren Eiseley points to the same experience in one of his remarkable stories. ''In Bimini, on the old Spanish Main, a black girl once said to me, 'Those as hunts treasure must go alone, at night, and when they find it they have to leave a little of their blood behind them.' ''[3] The process of transformation is not without pain. In becoming open to all that is new, there is the pain of letting go of all that is old. Sometimes the things that hurt us the most are the hardest to discard. The promise, however, is that in the struggle—that ongoing, ever-changing struggle for growth—God is always present. Through him we are transformed.

ENCOUNTER WITH THE STORY

If the process of transformation is born out of struggle to come to terms with oneself, it is deepened by a continuous encounter with the story that shapes our faith. A living faith is not something we have to carry; it carries us. It is lived dialogue with the Lord, nurtured and deepened by the impact of those ancient themes and images through which the Person of Christ is made known. Christian meditation leads us into personal encounter with the Lord. It opens up the deep places of our lives to the movement of the Spirit so that the Christ of the Gospel may permeate not only our rational processes, but those realms in which dreams and intuition are born.

The Christian journey begins with a personal decision to live one's life within the context of a particular story. The story we affirm is the story of redemption that reaches its climax in the death and resurrection of Jesus Christ. The reasons for making such a decision (often experienced as a combination of many decisions) are immensely varied since they involve all the conscious and unconscious material that makes up the human personality. To say "yes" to the Christ is a way of entering into a story which gives meaning and rootedness to our experience and links us indissolubly with that vast family of which we are a part.

Because we are all different, we respond to the Christian story in different ways. A theme or image that stands out for one person is not necessarily a predominant theme for someone else. As I look back over my own life I realize how central the story of the Prodigal Son has been for me. For me the story embodies themes that are fundamental to my life experience. I first heard the story of the Prodigal Son as a little boy, probably in a Sunday school class on one of those rare occasions when I attended. I have heard the story and told the story many times since. It is a story which, over the years, has become deeply embedded in my consciousness, touching such things in my life as my own search for a father, my own struggle for identity, my own attempts to gain mastery over the destructive forces within me, and holding these things up to the light and power of a loving God. The story of the Prodigal Son is the story of a person who finally backs away from the need to control his own destiny and in repentance cries out for a relationship which will transform his life. And as we all know, before the words are uttered, the relationship is offered.

It was at a time in my life when things were not working out that I encountered this story at a new depth. At a time when I felt most unworthy, I came to know that my worth was assured. There was nothing I could do to win this or earn this—indeed, like the Prodigal Son, I had done the very opposite. All I could do was to own the pain that was within me and turn to Him who reached out for me. In the very depth of my being I knew I was forgiven. I knew that my worth was affirmed unconditionally by the love of God. The words which I suspect came to the Prodigal came also to me: "You are forgiven. You are loved. You are worthy in the sight of God. No matter what happens, this affirmation will never be withdrawn. Go and live as becomes it."

Since that time this initial experience of the transforming power of God has been deepened and nourished by many sources although, admittedly, there have been times, even long times, when I have lost touch with it. The story of Jesus and Zacchaeus, the woman taken in adultery, the story of the Passion itself, all point to this profound truth in the Christian Gospel: life, self-worth and meaning are the gifts of God which come to us in faith. The development of faith is a combination of personal experience, biblical story and theological interpretation all woven together to form a crucible in which faith is deepened and nourished. My own personal experience of justification has been deepened by my encounter with Paul's Epistle to the Romans, with Paul Tillich's great sermon, "You Are Accepted," and by a thousand conversations with others who have shared my journey. Everyone responds to the Gospel in ways that are appropriate to his or her experiences. For me, the great affirmation of our fundamental justification by the Passion of Christ has been the theme that has been central to my own struggle for a meaningful faith.

SUSTAINED IN COMMUNITY

Transformation is born out of struggle. It is deepened through continuous encounter with the Word of God. It is sustained by a life lived in the community of faith. I am aware now how much the early years of my Christian journey were marked by my struggle to overcome the loss of my father who died when I was eight. Of critical importance in that struggle was the ministry to me by a clergyman who allowed himself to serve as a father substitute. While in high school, I was invited to assist him as an acolyte at the early Sunday service. My contact with the Church prior to this had been minimal, and it remained so for a while even after this year was over. But something happened, nevertheless. It was partly the mystery of the liturgy. It was partly the sense of being different. It was partly the great feeling of well-being with my mentor at breakfast when the service was over. Whatever happened, it has never left me. Something was touched deep within me and a change took place—a change that has been sustained by countless people countless times since.

Transformation is never a solitary experience. It takes place in relationship to others who in their own lives are visible witnesses to the presence of Christ in the world. It happens in worship as we gather with others to act out the myths and stories that embody our faith. It happens as we are caught up in "the story" by which the Christian community is shaped and nurtured. It happens as we encounter another human being at a level deep enough to break us loose from old ways of thinking and doing. The point is, the experience of inner transformation is deeply rooted in the shared experience of others who have chosen to walk a similar path. It is, as has been said so well, "learning to live by love—learning to be persons in community with other persons."[14] For better or worse, Christianity is indissolubly bound up with that community which we refer to as the Church.

THE AUTHORITY FOR MINISTRY

The Christian journey, therefore, is fundamentally a communal experience. The process of inner transformation, by its very nature, leads us more deeply into a sense of solidarity with the human family of which we are a part. Once the awareness of this solidarity begins to make its claim upon our consciousness, we are no longer solitary persons forever seeking the illusory excitement that comes from "doing our own thing," but persons in community seeking to break through those inner barriers that separate us from the human family.

In their "Second Letter to the People of God," the brothers of that remarkable ecumenical community in Taizé, France call upon the Church to once again hold up for the world a vision of human community—to become a parable of solidarity. Such a parable, they plead, would serve as a beacon of hope in a world where hope has become an increasingly rare commodity. A living parable will emerge when Christians of differing persuasions lock hands across the world on behalf of those who are without hope. Such a parable will involve a group of people struggling together for the goods of the earth to be rightly shared, persons willing to feel the pain of political oppression and torture in order to hold up another way for all the world to see.

"Everywhere new beginnings, new awakenings are discernible in the Body of Christ," states the letter. "If the Church gives up all that is not absolutely essential, if she resolves to be nothing but a servant of communion and of sharing in the midst of humanity, she will play her part in healing the wounds of the human family."[5] The question, of course, is as old as the prophet Isaiah. "Whom shall I send? Who will go for me?" (Isaiah 6:8) This was God's question to the prophet. And the echo lingers still. Are there people in the world, believers and would-be believers, who have tasted enough of the power of human solidarity to be willing to give themselves in faith?

Certainly both at the heart and on the fringes of our churches there are persons who are willing to give themselves to more than is generally offered; persons willing to learn again what it means to pray and to love and to live in ways that enable them to become solutions to the world's problems rather than unthinking contributors; persons willing to live life differently because at the core of their being they believe that life can be different. It is out of this kind of vision that authentic inner disciplines can emerge. They have nothing to do with whether we are ordained or not ordained, whether we are busy or not busy, whether we are secular or pious. It has to do with a view of life that sees in Christ the answer to human pain and hopelessness.

Ultimately there is only one authority for ministry. That authority is Jesus Christ. When laity claim they cannot exercise ministry in the Church because they lack authority, my immediate initial response is, "Who says?" The authority is there. It has been given in baptism. No one can take it away; no structure, no institution, no church, no clergy can take away that which is fundamental to who we are in Christ.

The authority for ministry is Jesus Christ. The Church only validates that authority and regulates it according to what seems to be needed. This is extremely important to the recovery of a sense of total ministry within the Christian Church. We are more than wanderers. We are a people under authority, engaged in a journey which leads not merely to a sense of personal wholeness, but to the wholeness of the human family. The way this journey is supported and sustained, therefore, is of critical importance, not only for ourselves, but for the future of the planet Earth. A bold claim, yes. But unless we are bold in our vision, there is great danger that we will settle for a world or a task that is too small.

The aim of this book is to embody this vision. It is an invitation to those who want more from life than they now possess, an invitation to share in the life and ministry of Jesus Christ. A life of inner discipline is not only the result of faith, it can lead to faith, just as we learn the meaning of love by loving. Our task is not to search for God, but rather to open ourselves to the reality of God's search for us. The initiative is His; the response is ours. He has loved us from the beginning and called us to share in His ministry to the world. This, we dare to proclaim, is the secret of human fulfillment. It is a matter of inner transformation, open to anyone who even tentatively is willing to say, "Yes!"

CHAPTER II

The Many Faces of Ministry

*Search for the Lord in His Strength;
continually seek His face.*

PSALM 105:4

In his autobiography, *Report to Greco*, Nikos Kazantzakis tells of a visit to a monastery in Crete which he made during a period of intense spiritual searching. "It was the wise Father Joachim who, clapping his hands as though I was a pullet, shooed me away. 'Return to the world,' he cried. 'In this day and age the world is the true monastery; that is where you will become a saint.' "[1]

Kazantzakis' words echo a call to ministry, a call to open our lives in such a way that they may be used in the healing of the world's pain. The ministry of the Christian Church is the ministry of Jesus Christ. It is a ministry to the isolation and the brokenness and the injustice that fragments the human family. "The spirit of the Lord is upon me," Jesus proclaimed to the synagogue in Nazareth. "He has sent me to announce good news to the poor, to proclaim release for prisoners and recovery of sight for the blind" (Luke 4:18–

19). We are called to share in this ministry. It is a call to be more than concerned citizens, more even than regular contributing members of a local congregation. It is a call to open our lives to the claim of Jesus Christ so that everything we do, we do in His name, as a part of His ministry to the world. "Though many are invited," Jesus said, "but few are chosen" (Matthew 22:14). I understand this to mean that the call is to all of us who "profess and call ourselves Christians," but that choice comes only after we freely respond. We are chosen for ministry when we are willing to take the next step.

THE DESIRE FOR SOMETHING MORE

Not long ago I happened to pick up the parish bulletin of a church in Washington, D.C., where a particular effort had been made to give support to the ministry of the laity. The leadership of this congregation had worked hard to develop an innovative program for the education of their adult membership, borrowing ideas from every source possible and, of course, creating some of their own. As I read the first line of this bulletin, I found myself especially intrigued. "Now that we have incorporated most of the best programs we heard about," it stated, "and now that so many people are ready to grow in new directions, the challenge is one of coming up with new and promising directions. Let me tell you my thoughts on this subject. For a long time I have had a day dream of a secular religious community

at St. Columba's. I don't know exactly what it would
look like, but it would allow lay people to have a discipline of spiritual growth, a small community of support, and multiple avenues of mission outreach. There
are just so many people who are coming alive in the
Faith and who deeply desire 'something more.' I do
not know what the 'something more' is, but my intuition is that if we could investigate other models of
religious communities, we might be able to develop a
healthy model of our own.''[2]

And so, for this particular church, the search began.
What struck me about this bulletin, however, was the
recognition that there are people in our churches who
are searching for ''something more.'' They may not be
the people that you would automatically think of. Indeed, they may be people whose Christian commitment is exercised primarily outside the life of the congregation, yet whose faith has brought them closer and
closer to an awareness of those things that give life
meaning and purpose. They are people who in a variety of ways have been claimed by the Lord Jesus
Christ, and who know it. For them the question of
''something more'' has a particular intensity.

It is when we are ready to ask the ''something
more'' question that we are most open to the call to
ministry. Ministry is more than doing good. It means
to serve in the Lord's name in ways—often small and
unnoticed—that enable Jesus Christ to act through us
for the healing of the world. Ministry, therefore, is not
something we do on our own. It is rather the response

to those "gifts" that each of us has been given, but which in most cases lie buried within us still waiting to be called forth.

CLAIMING OUR GIFTS

"In each of us," writes Paul to the church at Corinth, "the Spirit is manifested in one particular way, for some useful purpose" (I Corinthians 12:7). The way in which the Spirit manifests itself within us is what we call "gift." Gift is the action of God which calls forth those special qualities that are needed for the Lord's work. The New Testament speaks of gifts of healing and wisdom and teaching, to name but a few. But there are also gifts of listening, caring, problem solving and personal witness. It is the work of the Spirit to activate these gifts for ministry. In one of his better known parables, Jesus tells of the three servants who invested the gold they had been given in different ways. One servant was given five bags of gold, another two, another one, "each according to his capacity." The servant with five bags put it immediately to use and doubled his investment. So did the servant with two bags. The man with one bag, however, took his gold and buried it in the ground because of his fear of risking what he had (Matthew 25:14–30).

Our concern here is with the servant whose gift was buried—the fearful one. It is a truth that, when we allow the gifts we have been given to be called forth in ministry, they are expanded often beyond our wildest dreams. But it is also a truth that for most of us fear gets in the way. Buried within each of us lie gifts that we have not used, gifts that are often lodged in that part of us that we most avoid. For the cerebral, thinking types, it might be the intuitive, imaginative side of ourselves that needs to be exposed to the activating power of God. For the ecstatics among us, the opposite might well be true. "It is inevitable," John Sanford writes, "that in the growth of our personalities, much that potentially is part of us will not be developed. . . . All this undeveloped self is the unlived life which for the Kingdom to be realized, must get into our life in a legitimate way."[3] It is no accident, therefore, that there is so much attention paid in the New Testament to the recovery of that which is lost. The Kingdom of God is like finding a coin that had disappeared or discovering a pearl of special value or the treasure that had been buried in the field. The point is, the gifts necessary for sharing in the ministry of Christ are available to us all, but without the willingness to risk opening the unused, guarded parts of ourselves to the action of the Spirit they will lie within—dormant and untapped.

The primary task of the local congregation is to enable persons to discover their gifts for ministry so that these gifts may be celebrated and developed. One way to go about this is to provide settings in which persons can share with one another those aspects of their spiritual journeys that reflect their exercise of ministry. In doing this, four questions seem to me to be particularly helpful.

1. What are the gifts that lie buried within us?

2. Where are we already doing ministry?

3. What are the theological dimensions of what we do?

4. How can we covenant with others for mutual accountability and support?

The first question is a deeply personal one. It cannot be approached superficially or with haste. Its aim is to help us uncover those unique gifts or talents that we have possessed for a long time, yet which never have been developed. No one else can identify these gifts for us. The discovery is a personal one, coming out of the discipline of reflective prayer. To ask this question of ourselves involves time for solitude and the courage to respond to the Spirit's deep probing. It requires that we give our imaginative and intuitive self free reign, so that those gifts that we do not see may surface freely and without restraint.

Urban Holmes, in his book *Ministry and Imagination*, makes the persuasive claim that the primary agenda of the ministry today is to enable people to rediscover or relearn their capacity for intuition and wonder. "The fact that religious experience is considered so rare a thing among us," he writes, "does not mean that God is no longer present, but that in our Western culture we have made so little of the imagination, intuition and wonder to discern within our culture the presence of God."[4] The discernment of our deepest gifts is an experience of encounter with God. When these gifts emerge, even tentatively, our task is to address them, to determine how they may be actualized, and then begin the process of putting them to use.

The second question—Where are we already doing ministry?—is aimed at helping us reflect on those gifts that have already been called forth, yet are still unknown and undeveloped. It is based on the assumption that we are already engaged in Christian ministry in a number of ways that reflect those gifts that are uniquely ours. To look at the things that we are already doing for others, things that stretch us or call forth the best in us, is but another way of identifying those inner resources that have been brought into play by the action of the Spirit.

One of the most effective ways of examining the nature of our ministries is through the use of a "critical incident." There are many ways of doing this, most of which involve writing out a description of an experience where we are called upon to make a decision that was difficult and about which we were uncertain or felt particularly vulnerable. As we follow this decision through, with the help of others, we are better able to see what gifts were being called forth and what was either enhancing or blocking their use. When a group of persons helps one of its members to identify his or her gifts of ministry, they are not only exercising ministry themselves, but embodying the very essence of Christian community. There is no more important work that a church can do than to enable persons to share their gifts for ministry and confirm what is offered by others.

The third question opens us up to the theological dimensions of the decisions we make. In approaching this question we might look first at the values and perspectives reflected in the various poles of our decisions. Then we can more accurately examine how the Christian understanding of creation or personhood or redemption are present in what we see. In one group that worked with critical incidents, a mother shared her pain in trying to relate to her daughter who was living with a man to whom she was not married. The daughter's worldview was quite different from her mother's, yet not without value and integrity. As the group explored these two different worlds, not only new understandings but new dimensions of ministry emerged.

"Christianity," says Hans Küng, "consists of the activation of the memory of Jesus Christ in thought and practice."[5] Jesus brought sight to all aspects of human blindness. He unmasked the powers, both internal and external, that hold us in bondage so that we may be free. He brought forgiveness to those ravaged by guilt, and new life to those without meaning and hope. It is this precise ministry that continues both in us and through us. It is the ministry for which our gifts have been given.

The final question has to do with building covenants of accountability and support. Like our Jewish brothers and sisters, Christians are people of the Covenant. We are the heirs of the New Covenant given to us in the death and resurrection of Jesus Christ. Covenant is a symbolic word. It signifies an agreement that has deep spiritual roots. To make a "ministry covenant" with another person is to say that you want to be held accountable for what you intend to do. With accountability comes also support. We need people who will stand with us so that we might remain faithful.

Covenant groups usually range in size from eight to twelve persons, meeting regularly for set periods of time. The aim is to provide a setting in which members can explore how their gifts might best be put to use with enough specificity as to determine whether or not what they are doing is actually worthwhile. One man I know developed a ministry to parents of young persons in trouble. It was a ministry which began one evening at a dinner party when a troubled father poured out his anguish to my friend who, in turn, found he was able to respond in a healing way. By sharing this with his covenant group my friend not only received suggestions about how his ability to listen reflectively might be developed, including, of course, further exploration into the meaning of family trauma and adolescent rebellion, but also help in how he might go about exercising his ministry in a more disciplined way. By stating beforehand what he intended to do, he was able to ask the group to hold him accountable. They not only agreed to do this, but also took on the responsibility of praying regularly for the success of his ministry.

Eventually all members of this particular group were relating to each other in the same way. One member developed a ministry within his business; another was concerned with a particular political issue; another with persons confined to nursing homes; another member of the group developed a ministry to single-parent families. In each case the area of ministry was spelled out, intentions were clarified and a covenant developed which provided accountability, support and regular prayer for the persons involved.

Ministry has many faces. It begins to happen when we discover that Christ lives in us. It is the direct result of an inner transformation that causes us to see the world with new eyes. Ministry is the fruit of the Gospel promise, but for it to deepen, it must be sustained both from within and without. The purpose of the four questions just discussed is to help this sustenance to take place in a regular and disciplined way. We are called to serve others in the name of Christ. Finding "something more" involves taking this ministry seriously and building an inner discipline that gives what we do both substance and depth. The remainder of this book will seek to spell out what such a discipline might involve. It is based on a theology of prayer that emphasizes our need to get in touch with what God is already doing within us. In this way we can begin to experience the rhythm of the Spirit which pulls us inward to listen, and then pushes us outward as persons with a renewed capacity to love. Genuine caring is born in solitude. There can be no authentic ministry without it.

THE RHYTHM OF THE CHRISTIAN
JOURNEY

Every summer my family rents a beach cottage on the shore of South Carolina. This place has a special meaning in my personal journey because it is where, with my wife and children (now grown), we have put down roots. Last summer as I was walking along the deserted beach early in the morning, interrupted only by an occasional cry of a gull, I suddenly became aware of the relation of my life to the rhythm of the sea. I'm sure I'd had such thoughts before, but on this particular morning something was different. I not only heard the sea rolling up on the beach, I felt the sea. I experienced deep within me the ebb and flow of the ocean's rhythm. It was an awesome experience because so much was happening to me. The rhythm of breathing, the rhythm of engagement and retreat, of work and play, of love and hate, of contemplation and action— all of these things were suddenly experienced as one. The moment passed, but the image remains. A life which shares in the ministry of Christ is a life in touch with that deep rhythm that is at the heart of all life.

A life of prayer that is divorced from the call to ministry is incomplete. But so also is a ministry that is cut off from the inner movement of the Spirit. The life in Christ is lived out in the tension between contemplation and action. It is a life of solitude and community, of withdrawal and intimacy, of movement within and movement without. The rhythm of ministry begins with our response to God's choice of us, and it continues as we begin to make those choices by which life is transformed. Ministry is born out of the awareness that there is, indeed, something more. It is expanded as we take the risk of thinking and acting in new ways, especially in ways that expose our own vulnerability. It is nurtured in the discipline of prayer by which, through the grace of God, Christ is indeed formed within us. Ministry is more than doing good. It is living our lives self-consciously in the name of Christ with the love and support of a community both behind us and with us.

CHAPTER III

From Ought to Thirst

As the deer longs for the water-brooks
so longs my soul for You, O God.
PSALM 42:1

Not long ago I asked a group of people to jot down the words that came to them as they sought to complete the sentence, "Prayer is . . ." As you might imagine, the responses were as varied as the people in the room. "Prayer is . . . talking to God . . . thanking . . . praising . . . being open to God . . . listening . . . reaching out . . . asking for help . . . difficult . . . neglected . . . more talked about than practiced."

Since these people were all practicing Christians, I was particularly interested in the latter responses, so I pushed a little further. "Prayer is something I believe I *ought* to do," stated one man, "but I find it never occurs unless I am in church or under particular stress." Summing up many of the statements made by others, a young woman added, "We all ought to pray more than we do, but somehow it just doesn't seem to happen in real life."

As I listened to these comments, I was struck by

28

how heavy this feeling of "ought" seemed to be, a feeling I could well identify in my own spiritual journey. As I listen to people struggling with the meaning of prayer for themselves, I become more and more convinced that the feeling of "ought" is itself the problem.

BEYOND OUGHT

A persistent sense of "ought" has a way of draining us of our creative energies. When related to the act of prayer, it places the emphasis solely on what we must do, usually by some extra-determined act of the will. On top of this, add all those subtle but powerful layers of guilt that our "oughts" have a way of producing, and before long any natural inclination we have to pray has been safely cut off and bottled up. At its deepest level, prayer is not something *we* do, but something which the Holy Spirit does *in* and *through* us. To say we "ought" to pray is like saying we ought to breathe. No one who has experienced it would dispute it; it just feels like a case of misplaced emphasis. Breathing is a natural part of the life process—the rhythm around which our vital functions are built. So also is the rhythm of prayer. It is the avenue to those deep places within ourselves where the Spirit is encountered. Prayer is our access to the mystery of life which lies just beyond our vision. It is, as Anthony Bloom writes, "born of the discovery that the world has depths."[1]

If we are serious about prayer, the place to begin or

indeed to begin again is not with "saying" prayers, but with exploring the depths of our own lives. The emphasis is quite important. It is not what *we* do that ultimately matters, but rather our discovery of what God is already doing with us and within us. Our task is to get in touch with "the Spirit who intercedes within us," to use St. Paul's words, "with sighs too deep for words" (Romans 8:27). To begin to hear and experience these "sighs" deep within is to discover that thirst which lies beyond "ought." Prayer is a life of action lived in openness to God. It is a rhythm of engagement and solitude, of action and contemplation that flows out of an ongoing awareness of that Spirit-led journey which is uniquely ours. "To those who keep in the way," writes the Psalmist, "will I show the salvation of God" (Psalm 50:24).

The upsurge of interest in the practice of meditation which we are experiencing from so many quarters is directly related to a thirst for a quality of inner awareness that moves us beyond "ought," and beyond dependence on the verbal. We are experiencing the deep need on the part of increasing numbers of people to discover the particular dimension of human life where the language spoken is that of symbol and image and intuition. For it is within this dimension of life that thirst is born. Modern technology has given the world solutions to problems that hitherto were deemed insoluble, but not without a loss. What is missing in the human psyche is free access to such things as wonder, and mystery—the classic avenues toward the experience of God. The cry that is emerging in these last years of the twentieth century is for a contemplative style of life which can feed and deepen our capacity for compassion, a style of life enriched by those meditative disciplines that keep us open to the deep places within us where dream and symbol and utter stillness become for us fresh vehicles for encounter with God.

THE WELL THAT IS WITHIN US

In the fourth chapter of the Gospel according to John there is a remarkable dialogue between Jesus and the Samaritan woman which points to the kind of prayer of which we speak. Returning home to Galilee from Judea, Jesus passes through Samaria where, tired from his journey, he sits down by the village well. The Samaritan woman approaches the well and is immediately confronted by Jesus, who asks her for a drink. It was shocking enough for Jesus, a male, to address a strange woman, but it was doubly shocking for Jesus, a male Jew, to confront a Samaritan woman. He says to her simply, "Give me a drink." "What! You a Jew, ask a drink of me, a Samaritan woman?" she replies, probably a bit defensively. But Jesus doesn't let the conversation drop. He talks to her about thirst and the promise of "living" water. "Whoever drinks the water I shall give will never thirst again," he says. "It will be like an inner spring always welling up for eternal life." "Sir," says the woman, "give me that water and I shall not be thirsty, nor have to come all this way to draw" (John 4:1–15).

Like all the Johannine stories, the story of Jesus and
the Samaritan woman is a story of many dimensions.
In the context of prayer, however, it makes a very
clear affirmation. There is within each one of us a res-
ervoir of spiritual energy that comes out of the very
depths of our lives. It is like a deep well that we can
draw from forever—a well that never runs dry. Its
source is the love of God. Its vehicle, the Christ who
dwells in us. Christian meditation is simply the discipline by which we drink from this inner well. It is for
this living water that we thirst. When we are in touch
with its presence within us, it has a way of pulling us
deeper. And as the rhythm of moving inward and outward is established, prayer is experienced as a beckoning from within. "Sir," said the woman, "give me that
water and I shall not be thirsty." Such is the promise
of the Gospel. It is the promise from which wholeness
comes.

A contemplative life style, a life which seeks in a
disciplined manner to embrace both engagement and
solitude, emerges out of three very fundamental faith
assumptions. First, we affirm that in God the entire
created order is connected. Secondly, we affirm that
God continuously seeks to engage us in dialogue. And
lastly, we affirm that there is a place within the human
psyche where God may be encountered and experienced. There is, of course, no way to prove any of
these affirmations. They are a way of looking at the
world that is basic to any contemporary theology of
prayer.

ALL LIFE IS CONNECTED

To say that in God all life is connected is to affirm the systemic nature of reality. "In Christ," writes Paul to the Colossians, "everything in heaven and earth was created, not only things visible but also the invisible orders of thrones, sovereignties, authorities and powers: the whole universe has been created through him and for him. And he exists before everything, and *all things are held together in him*" (Colossians 1:16–18). Every thought or action on one person's part releases energy that affects the entire system in which the human family coexists, just as one intervention within the natural order affects the ecological balance through which life on this planet is sustained. It is in this context that we pray for others. In so doing we participate in the creative energy of God by which all life is connected and sustained.

There is an interesting story told in St. Luke's Gospel about an encounter between Jesus and a woman who had been hemorrhaging since she was twelve years old. The woman sees Jesus moving toward her through the crowd and manages to get close enough to touch His garment without being seen, hoping that in so doing she might be healed. The response of Jesus is quite abrupt. "Who is it that touched me?" he cries out. The disciples are startled and somewhat confused by the remark, given the fact that the street is jammed with all sorts of people who are pushing and shoving their way along. But Jesus insists. "Someone *did*

touch me, for I felt that power had gone out of me."
Whereupon the frightened woman comes forward and
acknowledges that in the experience of this power, she
has been cured. "My daughter," He says, "your faith
has cured you. Go in peace" (Luke 8:43–48).

No other healing story deals with power or spiritual
energy in quite the same way. It suggests that the life-
giving power of God is available to us in very concrete
and specific ways when we are in tune with the movement of God. I have a friend who tells of waking up
suddenly in the night with an overwhelming sense of
being cared for by someone he has not seen in years. In
making contact with that person, he discovered that on
that particular night this person had indeed been praying for him. The important issue here is not how this
happened or, indeed, if it happened in the way it was
perceived, but rather how the story indicates that all of
creation is linked up in ways that are beyond human
comprehension.

My friend's story and the Gospel story suggest to
me that, when I pray for someone who is ill or in trouble, energy is set in motion in the same way that rip-
ples are produced when a stone is dropped into a
smooth pond. This is the meaning of intercessory
prayer or prayers of petition. They are expressions of
our solidarity with one another and with the entire
created order. The great news of the Gospel is not that
each of us is separate and unique, but that in Christ we
are indissolubly linked with the entire human family. It

is in the celebration of our solidarity as broken people in need of healing that compassion is born.

Praying for others, therefore, is more than offering up words to God in the hope that they will be heard. Intercession is an affirmation of the interconnectedness of creation, a way of linking up with the life-giving power of God. To pray for another person or for a situation that is beyond our control is a way of participating in that which is fundamental to our life in Christ, the mystery of our solidarity with others.

OUR ENGAGEMENT WITH GOD IS DIALOGICAL

In the same manner, when we affirm that God is continuously engaging us in dialogue, we are affirming something which is fundamental about life itself. It is "in the signs of life which happen to us that we are addressed," Martin Buber once wrote.[2] Every event, every encounter carries within it the potential for an encounter with God. And as these events pass and are carried in memory, the potential for dialogue remains. Prayer, therefore, involves both encounter with events in the present and dialogue with those memories that connect us to our past.

The ways in which human beings experience God are immeasurable. God addresses us in accordance with who we are and where we are at any one particular moment. We experience Him as presence, ecstasy, judgment or insight, to name some of those modes of address that are most familiar. Although there are times when God addresses us in the midst of solitude, more often than not, His address is mediated through people. The Gospel speaks of our encounter with *the* stranger—the hungry and the thirsty and the imprisoned—through whom Christ chooses to reveal himself. The encounter could be a casual conversation or an experience of great intensity. Whatever the mode, something special happens, as if a door were opened within us and we allowed the other to enter. For a moment we are able to see things differently. There is a burst of creativity or insight that suddenly gives a new dimension to how we think and what we see. Faith tells us that these moments are neither coincidence nor self-induced. They come from outside ourselves in a way that seems to address something deep within us. They are, we believe, the experience of God Himself.

In most instances these encounters occur so suddenly that there is little time for reflection on what they mean. The reflective process which comes after our experience of encounter is a way of deepening the dialogue, especially when it is done on a regular basis in the context of meditation. Reflection on life experience becomes itself an act of prayer because it seeks to take seriously the address of God. It can be facilitated by the use of a journal in which each day we simply note these encounters which seem to have particular significance. Writing it down this way enables us to go back to the incident later and to experience it again in the spirit of prayer.

This process has a way of loosening up the soil of our lives so that more and more can be included in what we normally think of as prayer. Sometimes we find that, what begins as reflection on an immediate event, has a way of opening up long-forgotten experiences that obviously still contain elements of unfinished dialogue.

As I began working with this process in my own life, I found that time and time again memories of my father would flood into my consciousness. At first the emotion of these memories—especially my grief over his early death—made them difficult to deal with. But gradually, without forcing them into my consciousness, I found that the dialogue could continue. Some days it meant writing out conversations with my father which seemed to bubble up from within. Other days it was merely the recalling of long lost memories in a context that enabled them to be healed. Finally, the day came when the conversation seemed to be finished and we were ready to say goodby in a way that had not before been possible. The dialogue with God embodied in this aspect of my spiritual journey was complete. The point is, all of this is prayer and, unless we find ways of bringing our finished conversations and buried memories into conscious dialogue with God, we cut ourselves off from the whole dimension of His address.

There is no aspect of our life story—no dreams, no memory, no experience of joy or pain—that does not contain the potential for encounter with God.

THE PLACE OF STILLNESS

Fundamental to Christian meditation is the faith assumption that there is within each of us a place of divine meeting. Jesus spoke of the Kingdom of Heaven that is within us, of the spring that wells up for eternal life. Others have spoken of our center, of that place of central stillness where God is experienced in a unique and personal way. "There exists some point at which I can meet God in a real and experimental contact with His infinite actuality," wrote Thomas Merton. "This is the place of God, His sanctuary—it is the point where my contingent being depends upon His love. Within myself is a metaphorical apex of existence at which I am held in being by my Creator."[3] This is the affirmation from which is born the call to embrace solitude in the midst of our often busy and harried lives.

Most people, when beginning the practice of meditation on a regular basis, are soon confronted with a sense that what they are doing is merely illusion or, at worst, self-hypnosis. How do we know that what we experience in those moments of stillness deep within ourselves is anything more than a projection from our own psyche? The answer, of course, is that we don't. The conviction that in the depths of our being we can indeed encounter the presence of God is an act of faith, but it is a conviction that has a way of validating itself through continuous practice. There comes a time in meditation when the awareness of God's presence, even when absent, is something we believe to be true.

The late C. S. Lewis, in a little known poem which he called simply, "Prayer," addressed this question of reality versus illusion with his usual profundity. His words bear serious reflection:

> *Master, they say that when I seem*
>   *To be in speech with you,*
> *Since you make no replies, it's all a dream*
>   *—One talker aping two:*
>
> *They are half right, but not as they*
>   *Imagine; rather, I*
> *Seek in myself the things I meant to say,*
>   *And lo! the wells are dry.*
>
> *Then, seeing me empty, you forsake*
>   *The Listener's role, and through*
> *My dead lips breathe and into utterance wake.*
>   *The thoughts I never knew.*
>
> *And thus you neither need reply*
>   *Nor can; thus, while we seem*
> *Two talking, thou art One forever, and I*
>   *No dreamer, but thy dream.*[4]

MORE THAN WORDS

Prayer, then, is more than saying words to God. "It demands," as Henri Nouwen writes, "a relationship in which you allow the other to enter into the very center of your person, allow him to speak there, allow him to touch the sensitive core of your being, and allow him to see so much that you would rather leave in darkness."[5] Prayer is that response to God that is beyond "ought"—a response to a thirst that comes from deep within, beckoning us to pause and to drink.

> *Come! say the Spirit and the bride.*
> *Come! let each hearer reply.*
> *Come forward, you who are thirsty;*
> *accept the water of life, a free*
> *gift to all who desire it.*
>   REVELATION 22:17

CHAPTER IV

The Sound
of the Still Small Voice

For God alone my soul in silence waits;
truly, my hope is in Him.

PSALM 62:6

In the story of the prophet Elijah's conflict with Queen Jezebel, there comes a time when Elijah fears for his life. In desperation he flees into the wilderness by himself where he finds a place to sit and pray. Overcome by a sense of failure and hopelessness as the events of his life close in on him, all he can do is pray for his own death. "It is enough," he says, "now, Lord, take my life for I am no better than my fathers before me." But death does not come. Instead, Elijah experiences new-found strength, as if fed by angels.

Sustained, he goes deeper into the wilderness, finally entering a cave where he experiences an overwhelming sense of the presence of God. He is told to "stand on the mount before the Lord," which he does. Here he becomes aware of tremendous power, like a mighty wind strong enough to push rocks before it; but God is not in that wind, nor is he in the earthquake or the fire which follow. Underneath all this turmoil, Elijah hears "a low murmuring sound," or as the King James translation puts it, "a still, small voice," which addresses the very core of his being. He listens and responds, for he knows himself to be addressed by the voice of God (I Kings 19:1–4).

The story of Elijah in the wilderness, with all of its rich symbolism and drama, can be seen as a description of one man's experience of meditative prayer. All the elements of meditation are present: a place of solitude, the journey inward, the awareness of the turmoil within oneself, and then the experience of utter stillness found beyond the turmoil, a stillness filled with the presence of God. The result of Elijah's experience is a renewed capacity to engage the world. "Go back," says the Lord, "and finish the work I have given you to do." Out of the depths he finds the power that is necessary for ministry.

LEARNING FROM THE EAST

Christian meditation comes out of these ancient biblical roots. It is a form of prayer that makes it possible for us to encounter God at the deepest level of our being. It is a way of bringing our entire life journey into dialogue with God to be saturated with His presence even at the unconscious level of our experience. For this reason, meditation is different from what we generally think of as prayer. It is a movement within that requires both discipline and method, as well as a clear understanding of whom it is we seek.

We are witnessing today a widespread interest in the practice of meditation, stimulated by the impact of Eastern religious thought and practice on our own country and on much of the industrial West. There are obviously many reasons for the popularity of Eastern practices, not the least of which is the ignorance most Christians have of the meditative disciplines that undergird their own tradition. It is a plain fact that few churches in recent years have included training in the art of meditation in their ongoing educational programs. As a result, people have looked elsewhere and have learned from Yoga and Transcendental Meditation practices which have opened for them new windows into the inner life.

Much of Eastern meditative practice can be easily incorporated into the secular West because it is a practice that can be undertaken without religious commitment. It is quite possible to meditate twice a day with the use of a "mantra" (a word or phrase repeated over and over again as an aid to concentration) without acknowledging the presence of God at all. It is at this point where Christian meditative practice differs from Transcendental Meditation or Zen. Although many of the methods are the same, the goals are quite different. The goal of Eastern meditation is total detachment; the goal of Christian meditation is detachment from external stimuli and dependency in order to become "attached" to the God who makes Himself known in Christ. Christian meditation involves self-emptying in order for Christ to be formed in us and our lives lived out in union with him.

Having said this, however, it is very important to affirm how much Christians have benefited from dialogue with the East. The difference between what in Zen is referred to as "satori" and what a Christian experiences through the practice of contemplative prayer (e.g., meditation without words, concepts or images) is a subtle one and needs to be treated with cautious respect. As William Johnston so clearly points out, "the silence, the void, the passive receptivity, the existential detachment, the descent to the core of one's being or to the still point—everything included in what I have called 'vertical meditation' can be found in many cultures and religions, so that a mystical dialogue is not out of question."[1] The difference, as has been stated before, is Christ. When reaching the still point, that experience of utter detachment referred to in so much of Christian mystical literature, we find not "nothingness," but Christ welling up within us, claiming us as his own. There is nothing quite like this in Buddhist thought; but for the Christian rooted in the Incarnation, the Person of Christ is central. It is He who in the silence leads us into the presence of the Father where, without words or images, we simply behold the mystery of that reality which undergirds all life, whose name is Love.

DEVELOPING A METHOD FOR OURSELVES

There are many paths to Christian meditation, all with some things in common, but differing according to tradition and personal preference. The method that is suggested below has been put together from several different sources after much trial and error. Its major criterion is that it works for me. It is a method that has allowed me to bring the nuances of my own inner journey into the presence of Christ and, at times, beyond. I am convinced that each person seeking to develop a meditative discipline needs to establish a path that fits his or her own particular personality or need. The only way to do this is to try various methods, making what adjustments are necessary, until a pattern develops that feels right. Obviously, this means giving enough time to whatever method you are using so that you honestly know what it is about, lest you end up bouncing from one discipline to another. In seeking a path, a spiritual guide can be invaluable, especially one who has examined various paths of meditation for himself or herself.

Broadly speaking, there are four stages in the practice of meditation, each of which builds upon the other. They can be described as:

1. the preparation,

2. the movement inward,

3. from the Son to the Father,

4. connecting with the world around us.

The lines between these stages are not fixed; indeed, there is often some movement backward and forward as the Spirit moves within us. The idea is not to establish a discipline by which we march inflexibly from one stage to another, but rather to develop a sense of flow which gently draws us inward, pausing occasionally to take in what we pass along the way. The secret to meditation is to constantly remember that, aside from providing a loose structure in which to move, it is not *we* who do the work, but "the Spirit who intercedes within us with sighs too deep for words."

THE PREPARATION

In developing a personal meditative discipline, two very practical decisions must be made: we need a regular place and a regular time. While there will be times when we need to make adjustments, as a general rule the discipline of meditation comes easier when we develop a dependable routine. I have a large cushion that I keep in an upstairs room I use as a study. Since I generally meditate early in the morning, the room is quiet and I can enter into solitude without interruption. Usually I allow about an hour for my discipline, which includes time for reading and reflection, as well as twenty to thirty minutes for the meditation itself. I also find it helpful before beginning to engage in a few minutes of exercise, which helps the body both to awaken and loosen up. The salutation to the sun, which comes out of the Yoga discipline, is easy to do and extremely helpful, but there are many other simple forms of exercise as well.

Preparation for meditation involves the mind and the body. The idea is to create a setting, both externally and internally, in which the whole person is offered to God. After a few minutes of exercise (which I must confess I sometimes omit), we begin with a moment of prayer, either spontaneous or written, as in a Daily Office. This can be followed by reading a few pages from one of the classics or a contemporary work on the spiritual life which serves to bring our minds into a meditative stance. Then we move to readings from the Psalms and the gospels, which place us squarely within our tradition and give us material to draw from in the body of the meditation itself. I have found it helpful to read a psalm a day in sequence and to stay with one gospel until I have worked my way through it, taking a paragraph or a few lines each day. Normally, when I have completed the reading, I will make a few notes in my journal, especially if a particular phrase or thought strikes me as important.

The final element in preparing for meditation is simply learning to relax. This is of crucial importance to the meditative art and probably more than anything else determines how quickly we will be able to "move within." There are many methods of relaxation. One way is simply to tense and relax our muscles, beginning with the face and working down. Another way is to actually talk to our bodies until they become responsive to the mind's lead. Beginning with the leg, we can say, "My left leg is heavy, I am relaxed," concentrating on the left leg as we repeat the phrase two or three times and then gradually moving up the body. The idea is to bring the body and mind to that state of readiness where concentration is not something we bring about by some extra determined act of the will, but a state which seems to emerge naturally as the energy of the body comes into focus.

THE MOVEMENT INWARD

The movement inward begins as we join with the movement of our breathing. We begin, as an ancient Zen master is reported to have said, by letting "the breath breathe us." As the body relaxes and our breathing begins to slow down, we focus our attention on the rhythm, counting slowly "one and two and three and four." The count corresponds to the intake of air. The "and" on the exhale, going up to four and beginning again. This discipline helps to bring the mind into focus as the rhythm of the breathing draws us inward.

After a period of time with the counting, I sometimes substitute a mantra, such as "Be still/and know/ that I/am God" (Psalm 46), or "Lord Jesus Christ/Son of God/have mercy upon me" (the Jesus Prayer), letting the phrases adjust to the rhythm of the breath. It is no surprise that the idea of "breath" is such an important concept in the Bible. It is, in a very real sense, the source of life and therefore associated with the Breath or Spirit of God. To be in touch with the rhythm of one's breathing is to be in touch with the rhythm of life itself.

By concentrating on our breathing, we will find that we are gently pulled inward. The process is sometimes referred to as "centering" or finding the place of inner silence. We move inward until we find a place that feels like our spiritual center. Sometimes it helps to imagine ourselves in a pleasant room where we feel comfortable and secure. The idea is to create a setting by the use of the imagination that makes it possible to experience the stillness from within. For some people, creating such an imaginary place is distracting. They do better focusing on a beam of light or simply allowing a center to form as their thoughts and energies come into focus. Avery Brooke suggests that, in learning the centering process, it is helpful to concentrate on an object—a rock or a flower which we can hold in our hand—reflecting on such questions as, "What have we here?" and "What does it mean?" and finally "What is God saying to me?"[2] Whatever the method, our aim is to find that center within ourselves where the experience of God is most immediate, where beneath the turmoil and the passion we can hear the "still small voice."

During this process of moving inward the mind is often besieged with a barrage of images of one kind or another. Sometimes they come as stimuli from our work-a-day world, reminding us of work we need to do; other times they come from deep within as bright colors or symbols. Generally, it is best to let these images simply pass through the mind as bubbles floating to the surface. If we fight them or try to "put them out of our mind,'' we merely use energy that is better used in moving inward. There are times, however, when a memory or an image or the recall of a dream emerges in the mind with such clarity that it literally demands attention. Something about it makes it quite different from what we normally experience as distraction and, therefore, it needs to be responded to quite seriously. This kind of material comes from the flow of our inner journey and can contain for us the address of God.

I have encountered persons in my meditation—sometimes unknown, sometimes out of my past—who have brought me insights of tremendous value. These persons who come to the surface of our consciousness are sometimes referred to as "wisdom figures" because they serve as vehicles of wisdom from our unconscious past and from what Carl Jung refers to as the collective unconscious of the human race. Conversations of this kind are inner dialogues that can profitably be recorded in a journal for further exploration, a process that will be developed in more detail in the next chapter.

The material from our inner journey is an integral part of the meditative process. It is important material in our dialogue with the Spirit, but like everything else in the Christian pilgrimage, it needs to be brought into the healing and life-giving presence of Christ. As these dialogues occur in meditation (and we need to allow enough time for them to develop—anywhere from three to ten minutes), we can bring them in our mind to the Person of Christ. This serves as a counterbalance to our often unrecognized narcissistic tendencies, keeping the Lord at the center of the meditation. Christian meditation is not simply another method for self-development. It is a living encounter with the Son who, through the power of the Holy Spirit, brings us into the presence of the Father. There is no part of our journey which is exempt from the encounter. We come before the Lord as whole persons seeking Christ in us, the hope of glory.

FROM THE SON TO THE FATHER

There is only one experience of God. It is the same God who addresses us, both in the events of our external life and in the silent places of meditation. We do, however, understand and express this experience in different ways, sometimes as judgment, sometimes as insight, sometimes as ecstasy, sometimes as utter stillness without form or content. I find it helpful, therefore, to think of the experience of God in the pattern expressed in the Trinity.

In the strictest theological sense, we cannot name God. He is beyond our capacity to name Him, for to name Him is to define Him. God is beyond definition. He is that mystery that undergirds and gives meaning to all existence, that creative force which holds together all that was, and is, and ever shall be. In Christian understanding, Jesus embodies this mystery whom we call God, while at the same time, pointing beyond himself to that which defies definition. "God is the source of my being," he says. "My Father and I are one. I have glorified Thee on earth by completing the work which thou gavest me to do; and now, Father, glorify me in Thine own presence with the glory which I had with Thee before the world began" (John 8:42, 10:40, 17:4–5). Throughout his ministry, Jesus continuously points beyond himself to the mystery of the Father.

This, I believe, is what also happens in meditation. We encounter the Person of Jesus by focusing on the events of His life, allowing ourselves to be pulled into these events until, in a very real sense, these events and the Christ who gives meaning to them, become present as a source of life and power. There are times, however, when we are drawn beyond these events, beyond pictures and images and concepts, to that sense of presence that cannot be defined or even comprehended, only known in faith. "It is," in the words of Thomas Merton, "a deep resonance in the inmost center of our spirit in which our very life loses its separate voice and resounds with the majesty and the mercy of the Hidden and Living One."[3] While this is, of course, not an everyday experience, neither is it an experience limited only to great saints and mystics. It is the fruit of contemplative prayer open to all who are serious about the disciplines of the Christian journey. It is the experience of being led by Christ to the Father.

Meditation on the gospels can take many forms. By the use of the imagination we can place ourselves within the gospel scene in an effort to experience all that is to be found there. Or, in a less structured way, we can read over a portion of the gospel narrative (usually before we begin the meditation prayer), and let a phrase or an image that strikes us lead where it will. In this way, material from our life journey is able to intermingle with the Gospel material so that in a very real sense, our story and *the* story become one and the same.

One night during the winter I was returning from the movies with my wife and one of my colleagues. During our time in the theater it had begun to snow until, by the time we were ready to drive home, the snow was so heavy you could hardly see your hand before your face. Just a few blocks from home we were met by an oncoming car which had lost control rounding a curve. There was nothing we could do. In an instant the car smacked into us and we faced the momentary terror of not knowing whether we were alive or dead. Thanks to God, none of us was seriously injured.

That night, after finally getting to bed, I tossed and turned in restless sleep. The next night I went to bed early and slept soundly until awakened in the early morning by a dream. I dreamed that I was cradling my father in my arms at the time of his death and I was both afraid and sad. Normally, I would have gotten out of bed and recorded the dream in my journal, working with it a bit in meditation. But on this particular morning, the resistance within me was almost overpowering. I did not want to deal with that dream because I was well aware that in the dream I was being confronted by the reality of my own death.

I have often read that you cannot fully face into your life until you have faced the fear of your own death. I don't doubt this for a moment, although I must confess I don't find it easy to do. I have never been able to bring myself to say, "Today I will face my own death," without feeling a bit stupid. But, on this particular morning, I knew something was going on within me that wasn't going to go away. I avoided the issue by skipping my meditation altogether.

The next day I began my morning by reading the passage from St. Luke's Gospel where Jesus tells Simon Peter that he will make him and the other disciples, "fishers of men." Jesus is teaching on the shores of the lake when the people begin to crowd in on him. In an effort to move away, he enters a fishing boat owned by Peter and asks him to push off a bit from the shore. When he has finished speaking, he says to Peter, "Put out into the deep water and let down your nets for a catch." Peter resists. He has fished all night and caught nothing. But then he goes ahead and does what Jesus asks, resulting in a boat literally swamped with fish. Peter is terrified! "Go Lord, leave me, sinner that I am," he cries out. And for a moment there is silence, no doubt broken only by the lapping of the water against the boat. And then the words come, deep and penetrating. "Do not be afraid!" Then Peter is told that he will henceforth fish for men (Luke 5:1–11).

Since I was reading St. Luke's Gospel in sequence, this particular passage happened to fall on the day to which I refer. I read the gospel slowly and carefully and then began my meditation. As I began to find my center, I was aware of all the thoughts and fears that were bubbling up within me—including the dream—but I stayed with the passage. The deeper I went, the more vivid and compelling the figure of Jesus became. The command to launch out onto the deep came through as an invitation to risk owning those deep places within my own life, including that dark side of me from which my dream had come. I stayed with it until somewhere deep within me I heard the words, "Do not be afraid!" and I knew they were addressed to me. It was as if they touched the very center of my being and set me free.

"It is easy enough to say that God is seeking us, and even to stress how central this understanding is to Christianity," writes Morton Kelsey. "But it is harder to realize that we have to prepare so that God can break through to us. Meditation is simply the way we prepare, setting up the conditions that can help make this possible. . . . [Meditation] is a way for us to unlock the door and come out from the places where most of us have been hiding."[4] It is in this sense, Kelsey points out, that meditation serves to prepare us for all kinds of prayer. It creates the awareness from which prayer flows.

CONNECTING WITH
THE WORLD AROUND US

Christian meditation is not an end in itself. "We should desire and engage in prayer," writes St. Teresa, "not for our enjoyment, but for the sake of acquiring the strength which fits us for service."[5] Our service is to share in the ministry of Christ for the healing of the world. I have found it helpful, therefore, to conclude each meditation first of all with a word of thanksgiving, followed by intercession for one person or a situation where there is need. I find that the experience of the meditation sharpens my sensitivity and brings my normally diffused energy into focus. Directed intercession simply makes this energy available for someone else. Because it has been empowered by the energy of Jesus (like the woman who touched his cloak in the crowd), it contains the power to heal.

In offering this intercession, I try to picture the person or situation clearly in my mind and focus all my attention and all the love I can summon on that picture, holding it for a moment as I ask God for his assistance. I am convinced that this kind of prayer does indeed make sense, not only because it allows us to care, but because it affirms that interconnectedness which binds all creation together and acts on that affirmation.

Meditation is an art. It is an expression of human creativity, empowered by God, that brings into play our rational processes, our imagination and intuition, our feelings and will into one disciplined act of prayer.

But like any art, it requires patience and consistent practice. There are moments in meditation that are rich with the awareness of God's presence. But there are also many other times, often occurring in long stretches, when nothing seems to happen. Some have referred to these periods as the experience of God's absence, for they are devastatingly real. When they occur, we would do well to heed the words of the thirteenth-century author of *The Cloud of Unknowing:*

Even though your physical senses can find nothing there on which to feed themselves for they think you are doing nothing, continue doing this nothing, and do it for the love of God. Do not give up, but labor on with great effort in that nothing with a strong desire and a will to have God whom no man can know. . . . And who is it that calls this nothing? Surely it is our outer man and not our inner man. Our inner man calls it ALL, for it teaches him to know the essence of all things, both physical and spiritual, with no special attention to any one thing by itself.[6]

Meditation, in its deepest sense, is not something we do; it is God working in us. It is the act of prayer that enables us to get in touch with that ALL which is within us, calling us into the depths where, in a still small voice, we are addressed: *"Be still and know that I am God."*

CHAPTER V

Inner Discipline
and the Use of a Journal

For my part, I will sing of your strength;
I will celebrate your love in the morning.
PSALM 59:18

In *Alice in Wonderland* Lewis Carroll writes of Alice talking to the cat:

ALICE: Will you tell me, please, which way I ought to go from here?
CAT: That depends a great deal on where you want to get to.
ALICE: I don't care where.
CAT: Then it doesn't matter which way you go.
ALICE: As long as I get somewhere.
CAT: Oh, you're sure to do that if only you walk long enough.[1]

Alice is a wanderer. She meanders through life hoping that life itself will provide her with the direction she seeks. But as we all know, it just doesn't happen that way. The meaning and direction of our lives emerge

out of the commitments we make and these only become clear as we take time to enter into them in ways
that take us beyond the obvious. The way we do this is
implied in the word "discipline." Discipline, in this
sense, is not something someone lays on us from some
outside place, but rather it is what *we* do to focus our
energy in such a way as to accomplish what *we* want to
accomplish. A spiritual discipline, therefore, involves
all the things we do to nourish our "in-Christ-ness."
The secret lies in developing a discipline which fits
the nuances of our particular personality and allows
us to stay in touch with the flow of our journey.

At the heart of any Christian spiritual discipline lies
a concept that we don't speak about much in our
churches today: the concept of obedience. For most of
us the word immediately conjures up thoughts of pas-
sivity, blind submission or the rules and regulations
placed upon us in childhood. In theological terms,
however, obedience is a covenant word. We are
partners in a covenant of love initiated by God. Jesus
lived his life in obedience to this covenant. Our obedience is our response to what he has done. The call to
ministry is a call to the kind of obedience that takes us
beyond the casual participation or the uninspired business so often associated with the Christian Church.
"Obedience," writes Jacques Ellul, "is an active
struggle with all that impedes the reality of the life in
Christ."[2] It is out of our sense of obedience that we
discover the motivation necessary for a disciplined
life. It provides the staying power that is required if we

are going to move beyond sentiment to the reality
which ministry demands.

THE ELEMENTS
OF A SPIRITUAL DISCIPLINE

Spiritual discipline consists of many elements, some
quite traditional, others often highly innovative. Whatever the elements, our own spiritual discipline will
emerge out of who we are as we enter into dialogue
with the movement of our journey and the traditions of
which we are a part. For many years the community of
Kirkridge in Bangor, Pennsylvania has published a lectionary (a series of selected Bible readings) which
suggests elements that might be used in developing a
discipline for ourselves. On a daily basis they include:

1.   Openness to Scripture till word or verse speaks
with power;

2.   Intercessions by name, with thanks and praise;

3.   Centering down in silence before God;

4.   Seeking to act out Christian claims about justice,
enemies, church, families, body-earth-air, intellect,
our own affluence.

It is the aim of the Kirkridge discipline "in everything
to celebrate Christian faith in joy, without compulsion
and without anxiety."[3]

Most Christian disciplines that are concerned with the inner transformation of the whole person would reflect the spirit, if not the content, of the Kirkridge lectionary. Henri Nouwen, for instance, suggests that there are three things necessary for a disciplined journey: "a contemplative reading of the work of God, a silent listening to the voice of God, and a trusting obedience to a spiritual guide."[4] Morton Kelsey would add participation in the historic ritual expression of Christianity and a concern for the development of the imagination, adding specifically the use of a religious journal.[5] In the chapter preceding this one we examined at some length the use of the imagination in listening to the voice of God. The chapter which follows will seek to explore the art of spiritual guidance. In the remainder of this chapter I would like to look in some detail at the use of a religious journal in developing and sustaining a spiritual discipline. In my own life I have found this helpful not only in keeping touch with the flow of my journey, but as an aid to the discipline itself. There is something about writing down the date of each day at the top of a page which, even if nothing else were added, helps to build the pattern necessary for an ongoing journey. In a very real sense, my journal becomes an extension of myself.

KEEPING A JOURNAL

The purpose of a spiritual journal is to facilitate the dialogue between what goes on in the external events of our lives and what goes on within. In this sense, a journal is different from a diary. A diary simply recounts external events and our reactions to them. The journal helps us to move deeper into the inner journey—that dimension of life where our own particular story connects with that transcendental dimension of reality which we call God. A journal can help us get a feel for the movement of our life as it unfolds in response to the inner prompting of the Holy Spirit. It helps deepen our awareness of where we have been, where we are now and where we seem to be going. As I have mentioned earlier, it also helps to strengthen the habit of daily meditation. If we have time for nothing else, simply writing the date at the top of a blank page reminds us that our day is in itself an offering.

The journal can be as simple or as complex as we need to make it. Dr. Ira Progoff of Dialogue House in New York has developed a very comprehensive form of the journal which serves as a resource for the psychological restructuring of one's life. The use of what Progoff refers to as the Intensive Journal goes hand in hand with a method of meditation that enables a person to move "beyond psychotherapy" to what can best be viewed as a "transpsychological" approach to the journey toward wholeness.

Progoff's insights and methods are invaluable resources for the spiritual journey, especially when linked to the heritage from which we come. I have drawn from these insights and sought to integrate what I have found beneficial into that discipline which makes most sense for me. My concern is not primarily with a psychological journal. I am interested in being able to hear more deeply God's word for my life in a way that is simple enough to be used in a life that is busy and full. To my mind, the secret of keeping a daily journal lies in one's ability to keep it both simple and flexible so that it does not become a weight, but rather a practical tool.

In the Book of Genesis, God says to Adam, "Adam, where are you?" (Genesis 3:9). The journal is our response to that question. What we write in our journals is written for ourselves. Because of our tendency to censor what we write if there is the slightest possibility others will see it, it is best to have an understanding with those around us that it will not be read. The journal is only as valuable as our freedom to express ourselves through it.

My own journal is kept in a 5 × 7-inch spiral notebook. Others have found a larger looseleaf notebook more helpful. I begin my journal each day by writing the date at the top of the page and then, usually after I have finished my meditation, making brief entries in one or more of the following categories, depending on what seems to fit:

1. Any insights or reflections that have emerged in meditation;

2. Notations regarding my spiritual journey: things that are concerning me, stretching me, deepening me, calling me forth;

3. Dreams and their meaning;

4. Something I have read or thought about that I would like to remember.

It is not necessary to respond to all of these points every day. The idea is to choose what fits and to be brief, remembering always that we are writing only for ourselves. Than at the end of each week we can read over what we have written (when appropriate, reading it aloud) and let it, our ongoing spiritual journey, be a part of our meditation.

RECORDING INSIGHTS FROM MEDITATION

On March 1, 1977, I made the following entry in my journal following a period of meditation which emerged out of my reading of the story of Zechariah in the first chapter of St. Luke's Gospel:

Zechariah loses his speech because of his doubt—gains it back again when he stands firm at the center of his person. When he says clearly and without equivocation, "His name is John," he feels like a different person. Zechariah's response moves him beyond fear which I need to work on in my own life. It is better not to speak than to speak without integrity (or apart from my center). I forget this when I need to impress somebody—or even to fill up time. Lord, help me with this.

In a quite different vein I made an entry on January 13th of the same year after an intense encounter in my meditation with St. Paul. The meditation had begun

with the words in the Gospel of John about Christ as
the "True Vine," but very soon became centered in
the idea of the life in Christ. As I entered into that idea,
the person of Paul emerged in my consciousness as one
whom I experienced instantly as a source of wisdom.
He spoke to me and I responded, not so much in an
auditory sense, as in the exchange of thoughts between
two people who are bound together in a moment of
incredible intimacy. The conversation developed quite
rapidly and naturally until, after a few minutes, there
was a pause. Borrowing from the method developed
by Dr. Progoff, I picked the conversation up again,
only this time in my journal. As I was still very much
centered within myself, the dialogue seemed to flow
without effort. This is what I wrote and how I wrote it:

J: I see you are a much earthier person than I previ-
    ously thought.
P: You're right. I'm afraid I often get misrepresented.
J: I am fascinated by your sense of what it means to
    be "in Christ," but am not sure what it means for
    me.
P: Sometimes I mean something very deep; some-
    times something which is going on every day. I
    have the feeling that you often get too intense
    about this. Let Him claim you. He will claim you
    just as surely when you go about your business as
    when you are meditating.
J: You can get pretty intense yourself.
P: I prefer the word passionate. I am passionate. And

that's what I want for you, Jim. Let yourself feel
more, bubble more, love more. This is the more
authentic you.

J: You really touch me—and I am grateful, although
it's been hard staying with this. Thank you.

P: Peace!

I share these two rather personal entries as illustra-
tions of how the journal can be directly related to the
practice of meditation. I have found Progoff's work
with the inner dialogue especially helpful. Following
his lead, I have at times written out dialogues with the
memory of my father, with a problem that confronted
me, with the Person of Christ, and with numerous
wisdom figures—sometimes known, sometimes un-
known—that became part of my meditation. In one
sense, these inner dialogues are conversations with
myself, but they are conversations which take place in
such a way and at such a depth that they become
unique vehicles for the spirit. If every encounter carries with it the potential for an encounter with God,
even when these events are carried into memory or
locked into the unconscious, the potential for what
Buber describes as the dialogue between I and Thou
remains. The use of the journal helps to expand this
possibility.

NOTATIONS ABOUT THE JOURNEY

"The psyche in a human being carries the unfolding
purpose of his life, but in a form that is difficult to

trace," Progoff writes. ". . . it begins on the level of
intuition as a semiconscious intimation of things to
come."[6] In order to be aware of the nudges of our
intuition, we can record brief descriptions of occur-
rences which seem to challenge us or trigger some special reflection. For me, these entries tend to revolve
around behavior patterns that recur again and again
despite my best efforts, or events that seem to open up
new possibilities. Certainly one of the most contemporary and poetic examples of this kind of journal entry
can be seen in Dag Hammarskjold's *Markings*. His
"markings" were, as he describes them to himself,
"signposts you began to set up after you had reached a
point where you needed them, a fixed point that was
on no account to be lost sight of."[7] Such a signpost
was noted on June 23, 1957, some four years before his
death:

Result and reaction—the intense blaze of your anxiety re-
veals to what a great extent you are still fettered, still alien-
ated from the One.
   However, don't worry about this or anything else, but
follow the Way of which you are aware, even when you
have departed from it.
   "Nevertheless, not as I will, but as Thou wilt."[8]

The value of this kind of entry, even in its most
awkward and ungrammatical form, is not so much in
its immediate content, as in its relationship to what
went before and what comes after. By reflecting on
what we have written, we are able to sense the movement of our lives in a new way both to give thanks and

to work through those things that block or divert our journey to Christ.

DREAMS AND THEIR MEANING

One of the most interesting results of the enlightenment on Western religious thought is the way it produced distrust of dreams as a source of divine revelation. It seems as if the more important dreams became to modern psychology, the more suspect they became to the Church. Such suspicion is ironic when you consider the place dreams played in the biblical experience of God. Obviously there is the same problem with a literal and uncritical interpretation of dreams as there is with a literal and uncritical interpretation of the Bible, but this does not negate their importance to the Christian journey. "Dreams," writes Morton Kelsey, "are like cartoons or parables. They signify something beyond themselves. They attempt to tell a meaning, or many meanings, by means of images, in much the same way that the cartoon artist expresses his meaning by the use of symbols."[9]

All of us dream, usually on an average of four or five times a night. We often don't remember our dreams simply because we have not developed the discipline of recall. Someone who is working with his or her dreams in a therapeutic situation generally has a high rate of recall; in most cases we remember our dreams simply because we want to remember them. One way to develop the capacity for recall is to write our dreams down as soon as we wake up. One person I know, in an effort to develop the discipline, kept a pad by her bed in order to write down a dream if she woke in the middle of the night. I, myself, have never been quite so eager. For me, the journal serves the purpose quite adequately. After noting the date in my journal, I simply write a very brief description of my dream if I remember it or want to record it, before moving on to my reading and meditation. In this way, the material of the dream can become a part of the meditation itself.

The secret of working with dreams is not to push them for some special meaning. Rather, it is better to nurture them gently, allowing the images and the feelings we have about the dream to emerge through their own energy. The idea is not to analyze the dream as if dissecting a frog, but rather to respond to the dream intuitively—letting it speak to us. Approach the dream with the question, ''Is there anything in this dream I need to hear?''

One morning in my journal I made the following entry:

Dream: I'm in the ocean looking for a great whale. Have on snorkling gear. Person I'm with (?) grabs a lobster and tells me to do the same, so that the lobster can pull me. I resist this, feeling uneasy, but then grab the lobster and push out into the deep. Soon aware that I am very far out and have lost my direction. I wake up. Afraid.

This dream marked a real turning point in my spiritual journey. I worked with it for several days both in meditation and through dialogues with the image of the whale and the feeling of fear. All of the elements in a dream are part of ourselves. What we experience is our psyche searching for wholeness, an experience which has profound spiritual implications. Unless we are interested in searching out all the psychological dimensions of our dreams (a discipline in itself), the simpler our response the better. Our aim is not self-analysis, but rather to look and to listen as deeply as possible for hints of the Spirit's work within us.

THOUGHTS TO REMEMBER

This category of journal entry is probably the easiest of the four I have suggested, yet often provides entries that we can go back to again and again. It simply involves noting sentences or ideas in our reading or conversation with others that struck us as important. The value of such an entry is not only that it helps us remember thoughts we would like to hang on to, but it also tells us something about our spiritual state at the time. What strikes us as important one day might not strike us at all the next.

My journal is full of phrases from the psalms and the gospels and quotes from various people I have read. One morning I wrote down, "When one takes God as he is divine, having the reality of God within him, God sheds light on everything. . . . He will be like one athirst with a real thirst, he cannot help drinking even though he thinks of other things.'' These are words from Meister Eckhardt's *Talks of Instruction*[10] that I have returned to again and again. When I first read them, they touched something deep within me. By reading them again I find I am often able to return to that place. The same idea applies to almost anything we read or hear. By recording those thoughts that are gleaned from the spiritual classics or more contemporary writing, we enrich our journey with the reflected wisdom of the ages.

A MATTER OF BREADTH AND DEPTH

Keeping a spiritual journal is a linchpin in the development of an ongoing discipline. When it becomes a burden, we need to adjust it or shorten it, lest it block the flow it is intended to reflect. A journal is a friend that needs to be trusted with gentleness and respect. It opens us up to the breadth of our journey and can help take us to the depths. It is what *we* make it.

CHAPTER VI

Companions Along the Way

Your word is a lantern to my feet
and a light upon my path.
PSALM 119:105

It is not easy to maintain a disciplined life. It is even more difficult to include, within the rhythm of one's life, time for regular meditation or work with a journal. The pace at which most people live produces pressures, both within and without, that make solitude feel like a luxury. Despite the overwhelming evidence that a balanced life which embraces solitude in a serious way not only causes us to work more effectively but makes it possible for us to live healthier and longer lives, we still feel uncomfortable giving this side of our life experience genuine priority. The reasons for this are often complex, involving everything from self-hate to a genuine struggle with the legitimate demands of the job we are paid to do. The solution, therefore, does not necessarily involve greater effort, but rather greater honesty coupled with the willingness to ask for help. Fundamental to the Christian journey is the knowledge that we do not travel alone. We do indeed have companions along the way.

72

Several years ago I was having a particularly difficult time living with the spiritual discipline I had established for myself. Instead of getting up and moving easily to the place where I generally spend my time alone, I experienced an almost irresistible urge to do almost anything rather than settle down into my usual pattern. One morning it was the newspaper. Another morning I found I was just puttering around the house in a rather aimless fashion intent on doing absolutely nothing of any consequence. This pattern kept up for several days, let up a bit, and then recurred. In an effort to get at what was going on—when I could finally admit that something *was* going on—I met with a wise friend whom I trusted and who I knew was serious about his own inner discipline.

After hearing of my concern, he probed a bit about what it was I actually did in the morning when my discipline was going smoothly. I shared with him my usual pattern—readings from both the Old and New Testaments, meditation and rather extensive entries in my journal. "It feels awfully elaborate for so early in the morning," he commented almost jokingly. I responded to his lead and began exploring my feelings about the discipline I was working with. I had to admit that it did feel rather heavy. "Why not simplify things a bit and see what happens?" he suggested.

I took his lead and began simplifying my early morning pattern—only one lesson of scripture, very brief notes in my journal—all in an effort to bring what I was doing into sharper focus. The result was as if someone had broken the log jam. The resistance subsided and I was in touch with the flow again. This would not have happened, at least not as rapidly, had it not been for my spiritual guide. This person, with whom I have met over the years, is in a very real sense a companion in spirit.

My relationship to my guide is a very special one. We rarely see each other on social occasions. Our object in getting together is to explore the often rather subtle movement of my spiritual journey. He, in turn, worked with another guide for himself, although in some relationships of this kind each person takes a turn at serving as a guide to the other. Admittedly, this is not a common practice among all Christians. For some, it smacks of an invasion of privacy. Others simply have not considered that such a relationship could exist. It can, and does. I know of nothing that is more helpful in sustaining and deepening our inner pilgrimage.

Spiritual guidance is an art aimed at helping people find what they need for serious Christian discipleship. It is, as John H. Wright suggests, "an interpersonal situation in which one person assists another to develop and come to greater maturity in the life of the Spirit, that is, the life of faith, hope, and love."[1] Traditionally, such an art has been referred to as spiritual direction, suggesting by this very name the model of the expert teaching the novice. I prefer the terms guidance or companionship simply because they place the emphasis, not on the authority of the expert, but on the shared experience of a fellow journeyer. It is my conviction that the art of spiritual guidance needs once again to become normative in the life of the Church in the same way that pastoral counseling and caring for persons within a congregation has been normative since the impact of the psychological revolution. Spiritual guidance need not be relegated to experts, although some people are more experienced than others. There is no reason why anyone serious about his or her own spiritual growth cannot be a companion and guide to someone else, given the necessary training and support.

There are many ways to begin a spiritual companionship. We can simply seek out someone who seems to share a common interest or someone we know to be serious about his or her own spiritual discipline. Often such a relationship develops after the shared common experience of a workshop or class devoted to spiritual growth. It might involve an intentional search. We are looking for someone who first of all seems to be interested in such things as prayer and the well-being of the human community. We are looking for someone we can trust, someone who is sufficiently on our wavelength to be able to talk about the inner life without feeling foolish. As one friend said to his would-be spiritual companion, "How about getting together for lunch to talk about what it would mean if we were to take Christianity seriously?" It might mean meeting with a few people before the right relationship develops. There is no set way to find a companion. We are asking someone we trust to begin exploring with us those elements of the life journey that are not usually talked about. Once the relationship is established, a regular time of meeting can be set and the companionship begun. If we are just beginning on a discipline, there is a real advantage in meeting every one to two weeks, although as our patterns are established meetings will probably occur every month or even every six weeks. The meetings usually last from an hour to one and a half hours.

The key element a spiritual guide can give to another is support. It is often hard to maintain a regular spiritual discipline. We get distracted or discouraged, or we begin to touch those deep places in our lives that, because of hurt or fear, resist exploration. The task of the guide is to help us focus on our strengths so that we can do what *we* want to do or, more accurately, what the Spirit wants to do in us or through us. Spiritual guidance is not psychotherapy or pastoral counseling or evangelical witness. It is a supportive relationship aimed at helping another person grow in "prayerful response to the Spirit." "The attempt," writes Fr. William Connolly, "will include the willing ear, may include advice, and may result in relief from anxiety and more respectful observance of law. But its primary goal is growth, the development of lived dialogue with the Lord."[2]

When serving as a spiritual guide to someone else, I try over a period of time to explore five areas that seem to me to be particularly important. These are:

1. the relationship between my companion and myself,

2. the ministry to which my companion is committed,

3. the discipline he or she has chosen to follow,

4. the process of the journey itself,

5. resources that might possibly be helpful.

The first area is obviously the key to the effectiveness of what goes on between us. Unless there is trust, nothing of consequence will happen. Trust emerges, I believe, when my response to my companion comes out of an awareness of my own journey, with its joy and its pain. I can be authentically present to another person in this kind of relationship only when I am authentically aware of the presence of the Spirit both within me and between the two of us. To strengthen this sense of presence, I find it helpful to begin our meetings with two to three minutes of silence, allowing us both to "center down." In this way we are able to engage each other from our own depths. I meet with my companion to give support and encouragement while making available my own journey. My aim, however, is not to impose what has worked for me, but to help the other person discover what is most real for him or her.

The second area concerns the use of time. The purpose of an inner discipline is to give substance and depth to those ministries we exercise in the world at large. If our relationship to Jesus Christ is being deepened in prayer, then it will affect the way we live. It will affect our values and our priorities and the way in which we respond to human need. We are called to share in the ministry of Jesus Christ. The way in which we covenant to exercise this ministry is fundamental to our spiritual journey and therefore needs to be considered in a relationship with a spiritual companion. Such questions as:

What priorities do you give in your life to the need for both work and play, compassion and solitude?
What seems to throw this out of harmony?
How does what you do reflect the ministry of Jesus?

These are obviously not exhaustive, but they do help link up our inner journey with the call to servanthood. Dag Hammarskjold made this point well: "In our era the road to holiness necessarily passes through the world of action."[3] One task of the spiritual companion then, is to help us keep the inner and the outer in balance.

The third area of concern is the actual content of the discipline we have undertaken—the pattern by which we formalize our ongoing encounter with the Spirit. Is it balanced? Is it rooted in Scripture? Is it adapted to the demands that impinge upon our lives? Does it allow time for the mind and heart to fully enter into silence? Are we staying with what we have chosen to do? If not, what is the nature of our resistance? The discipline we undertake is the key to our inner journey. It is the task of the spiritual guide to hold us, in a supportive and enabling manner, accountable to what we have chosen to do.

The fourth area of attention between spiritual companions is the journey itself. As the habit of daily meditation begins to establish itself, there is an increased sense of meaning and direction to our lives. Clues about this direction begin to emerge within meditation and in the thread that connects up our journal entries, including our dreams. After a relationship has been fully established, a spiritual guide can help us pick up these clues at times when we are unable to see them ourselves.

There was a period in my journey when I was responding to every new spiritual movement emerging on the American scene. I was reading the writings of the Sufis, literature dealing with Zen and Tibetan meditation, as well as new explorations in transpersonal psychology. After many months of this, I found it more and more difficult to find any focus in my meditation. My dreams were full of imagery that seemed wild and disconnected. My guide began to sense that, spiritually, I was all over the map. He made some suggestions that helped me begin to recover my sense of direction. He saw what I was unable to see. The issue, of course, is what or who we seek in meditation. If it is excitement—a "high"—our journey will reflect this goal. If it is the Lord of the Scriptures, He will make

Himself known. The key is to stay in touch with the direction that our journey takes so that we may be open to the signposts along the way.

The fifth area of importance for spiritual companions involves the resources that are available to us in our journey. The most obvious, of course, are books that we ourselves have found helpful. In starting off with a companion who was just beginning a disciplined journey, I would suggest all the things written to date by Elizabeth O'Connor and Henri Nouwen.[4] These two writers, from quite different traditions, provide an approach to spiritual discipline that is comprehensive, balanced and engagingly readable. Beyond this, the list is endless and important to pursue. If we are blocked emotionally, it might be that we need a therapist or pastoral counselor who can help us move beyond the impasse that is blocking us. The spiritual guide is not a therapist and must guard against letting the relationship to his or her companion become a therapeutic one. The task of the spiritual guide is to provide support and appropriate assistance by which a person can build on his or her own strength and initiative in response to the Spirit.

When we are ready to begin working with a spiritual guide, the question which obviously confronts us is "Where are we going to find one?" This area of the Church's life has been so neglected, however, that such a question is not easily answered. To begin with, we must accept the fact that spiritual guidance is not everyone's cup of tea. Effective guides are persons who have worked enough on their own emotional and spiritual development to be able to relate to others without projecting their own needs upon them. Given this, the issue revolves around the degree of our own personal commitment to the Lord and to the movement of our own inner journey. This suggests some knowledge and practice in the art of meditation, a personal theology of prayer that is balanced and in touch with the tradition, and an established discipline for ourselves. It would be important to have developed good listening skills since the key to effective support is the ability to be fully present when another speaks. And, of course, it would be important to know what spiritual guidance is, and what it isn't.

There are persons available within the life of the Church who, with support and training, could very effectively exercise this kind of ministry. No training is any more important or more desperately needed. However, until there are persons ready within the Church to exercise this ministry, we will do better developing a relationship with someone we trust, learning from one another as we go along.

Most of the great classics of the Christian tradition were written as resources for spiritual direction. Obviously, they reflect the age in which they were written, exhibiting both the insights and the limitations of their eras. The early Desert Fathers of the third and fourth centuries, for instance, seem bizarre in their asceticism, but they nevertheless have given to future generations incomparable insights into the meaning of solitude. St. Teresa of Avila's writings in sixteenth-century Spain provide as clear a guide to the contemplative journey as has ever been written, but her work must be viewed with a critical eye toward those ascetic practices which we now understand to be less than helpful. Teresa's *Interior Castle* gives a step-by-step account of the movement of the human spirit toward union with God. It is similar in spirit to the great work of her contemporary, St. John of the Cross, but, to my mind, easier to read and therefore more useful to someone just beginning a study of the inner journey.

In addition to these, I have found several other classics particularly valuable in equipping me to be more sensitive, not only to the subtleties of my own journey, but to those of others as well. The first is Meister Eckhardt's *Talks of Instruction* written in the early fourteenth century. Here is a work of invaluable practical help as relevant today as the day it was written. There are times, Eckhardt is quick to own, when in meditation the mind goes astray and there is a sense of having lost God. "I can give you no better advice," he says, "than to find God where you lost Him."[5] His approach to the spiritual life is remarkably open-ended and flexible for, as he reminds us, "God never tied man's salvation to any pattern."[6]

Another classic that can serve as a valuable resource in developing the art of spiritual guidance is Francis de Sales' *Introduction to a Devout Life,* written in the early part of the seventeenth century. The value of this book is in its step-by-step instruction in the practice of imaginative meditation. Its language is flowery and some of the disciplines it suggests are not particularly helpful; but, because it was written by a wise spiritual director to one beginning to develop the disciplines of the spirit, it serves ably as a description of one kind of path. A good balance to the approach of de Sales' work, however, might be the thirteenth-century classic, *The Cloud of Unknowing,* simply because its emphasis is on nonverbal meditation, reflecting some of the interests in the contemporary American scene brought about by the impact of Zen.

A work that I have found particularly helpful comes from a different stream within the Christian tradition. This book is *The Way of the Pilgrim,* a classic of Greek and Russian spirituality which describes a method of meditation very different from that developed in the West. This method is developed further in much of Orthodox spiritual writing, but nowhere any more lucidly than in an anthology compiled by Igumen Chariton entitled *The Art of Prayer.* This anthology is particularly useful, not only as a survey of Orthodox spirituality, but as an invaluable resource for developing one's own theology of prayer. As the eminent sociologist Max Weber once wrote, "Tradition is the authority of the eternal yesterday." Nowhere is this any more true than in coming to understand and appreciate the infinite variety and wonder of the journey in Christ.[7]

Like any process that enhances personal growth, spiritual guidance is an art. If this art is once again to become normative in the Christian Church, we need to develop individuals who can be guides to spiritual guides. Some clergy, because of their training and temperament, are ideally suited to perform this function; others are not. Nor is ordination necessarily a prerequisite. It is good to recall that Evelyn Underhill and Baron Von Hugel, two of the great spiritual guides of our era, never attended a seminary or needed to. If we are to raise spiritual guides within congregational life, we will need more people who are familiar with the development of spiritual direction within the Church and are versed in what generally is referred to as ascetical theology. But more important still is the need for more and more persons who are committed to a disciplined ministry in the Lord's name and able to make their own journey available to others.

CHAPTER VII

The Spiritual Journey and the Local Church

You speak in my heart and say, "Seek my face."
Your face, LORD, will I seek.

PSALM 27:11

The local church has two primary functions. It gathers together for the worship of God and it provides the structures necessary for people to learn how to identify and use their gifts as participants in Christ's ministry to the world. We gather and we scatter in obedience to the Lord, whose ministry we share. The disciplines of prayer are necessary for both these functions. Prayer opens us to the mystery of God. It is the process in which our journey is laid open to the transforming work of Christ. Christian ministry is rooted in this process, which stands at the very center of the Church's life.

In this final chapter, we shall seek to address three areas in which the local church can assist people in building disciplines for Christian ministry. First, we will look at the kind of environment which needs to be created if individuals are to be encouraged to develop meaningful spiritual disciplines. Secondly, we will briefly explore the relation of worship to the deepening of the inner journey. And lastly, we shall seek to examine some ways in which a church might go about training persons in the disciplines of prayer, pulling together in a manageable fashion some of the approaches to a disciplined ministry developed in this book.

The task of the Church, as the Epistle to the Ephesians states so clearly, is "to equip God's people for work in His service, to the building up of the body of Christ" (Ephesians 4:12). No program, no matter how strong, can do justice to this task. We can, however, help build the kind of community where ministry is taken seriously and where the richness of the gifts we have been given can be celebrated and shared. We can help build the kind of community where men, women and children, called to share a common discipline, might be companions along the way to one another. It is a task worthy of our best efforts.

CREATING A SUPPORTIVE ENVIRONMENT

Every congregation has an environment that is unique to itself. This environment is the aggregate of all the norms, rituals, beliefs and customs that influence the way people think and act within the life of the Church and is, therefore, of major importance to a person's motivation for ministry. The environment in some churches produces behaviors that are guarded and cautious, while in others the environment seems to encourage risk and deeper personal involvement. The issue of environment, therefore, is of particular importance in encouraging persons to be more serious about spiritual disciplines.

There is a strain within the life of the Church which would confine the exploration of prayer to an environment where people speak only in biblical language, with soft voices and slightly lowered eyes. It is an environment where anger is denied in the name of "being nice," even at the cost of personal integrity, and where sexuality is viewed primarily as a source of threat. This is the kind of environment in which Christian spirituality has all too often been nurtured—an environment, incidentally, which is neither spiritual (in the best sense of the word) nor Christian.

"Spirituality" describes the response of the whole person to the action of the Spirit within us. A healthy Christian spirituality can affirm the sensuousness of the human body with the same vigor that it gives to the ecstasy of prayer. Pleasure is not the enemy, be it sexual pleasure or the pleasure of human creativity. It is *all* the expression of that energy which, in ministry, we place in the service of the love of God. A congregational environment which is conducive to the establishment of meaningful and healthy spiritual discipline must work at widening its norms so that such things as conflict, sexuality and concern for the world are seen as central to the Christian enterprise. Prayer, ministry and one's own personal journey are intimately connected. They need to be understood as expressions of the whole person growing in responsiveness to the needs of the whole world.

The question of environment is, therefore, crucial for the local church. Prayer must be removed from its stained-glass surroundings and placed in the service of Christ's ministry to the world. Environment, however, also has a personal dimension. Part of the reason for establishing a spiritual discipline is to create an environment within ourselves that enables prayer to undergird everything we do. Our task is to extend the spirit of meditation throughout the day so that to an ever-increasing degree we become, in every sense of the word, "Christ-conscious." This is what Christian faith is about. It is, in one sense, the process by which Christ is formed within us, the process which gave rise to Paul's assertion that it was no longer he who lived, but Christ who lived in him.

There are many ways to maintain and deepen this kind of environment. The disciplines referred to throughout this book are geared to this end, as is our participation in the life and worship of the Christian community. There is one discipline to which I have alluded, however, that deserves further mention. It involves the use of what, in Eastern Orthodox Christian circles, has come to be known as "the Jesus Prayer."

PRAYING THE JESUS PRAYER

On the 24th Sunday after Pentecost I went to church to say my prayers there during the Liturgy. The first Epistle of St. Paul to the Thessalonians was being read, and among other words I heard these—"Pray without ceasing." It was this text, more than any other, which forced itself upon my mind, and I began to think how it was possible to pray without ceasing, since a man has to concern himself with other things also in order to make a living.[1]

So begins *The Way of the Pilgrim*, one of the great classics of Eastern Christianity. Its emphasis is on a spirituality which is geared to the rhythm of the Christian pilgrimage lived out in the world. Its method is the Jesus Prayer—"Lord, Jesus Christ, Son of God, have mercy on me"—repeated silently over and over again in conjunction with the rhythm of our breathing until it becomes an unconscious effort, a "prayer of the heart."

I have found the use of the Jesus Prayer extremely helpful on those mornings when, for one reason or another, I skipped my time for formal meditation. It is a prayer that I use often when driving long distances on the highway, or waiting in a car for a traffic light to change, or when standing in line, or when preparing to meet a situation or a person when some anxiety is involved. "Lord Jesus Christ, Son of God, have mercy on me. Lord Jesus Christ, Son of God, keep me firmly within your covenant," as the root of the word *mercy* suggests. The prayer begins with the words of the prayer being formed on the lips. In the course of time the prayer becomes more inward, acquiring a rhythm of its own, until finally, in the words of Timothy Ware, it "enters into the heart, dominating the entire personality."[2]

Obviously, this does not happen overnight. The full internalization of the Jesus Prayer is a lifelong effort, but even to begin establishing a rhythm helps to sustain the contemplative spirit in the midst of those pressures that most of us face in a normal day. The Jesus Prayer represents a very important principle in Christian spirituality. Prayer is not so much an act as a way of life, sustained from within and without by those environments which encourage us to take our inner journeys seriously.

WORSHIP AND THE INNER JOURNEY

At its core, religious experience is concerned with the transcendent. This is not to suggest that religious experience is unrelated to the realities of life, but that it concerns a dimension of life that cannot be neatly summed up in the scientific categories to which we are accustomed. There is an intuitive and symbolic level to human experience where change can be just as radical as that produced by a new technology, and sometimes even more lasting. I think we need to be quite straightforward about this. There is a tendency in Western Christianity to shy away from anything which is not functional or pragmatic, hence our discomfort with such words as *spiritual* or *mystical* or, in some circles, even the word *God*. But the plain fact is, something does happen to people as the result of religious experience. Changes occur deep within the psyche that have a profound and lasting effect on the way we live out our lives. Nowhere is this process of inner transformation more active than in the experience of corporate worship.

The Grubb Institute in London has been engaged in some fascinating studies on the place of worship in the process of human development. Working with the need they see for all persons to "regress to dependence,"[3] they are engaged in some very important studies of the relation of religious faith to personal growth. In this view, each one of us is constantly involved in a process of oscillation from extra-dependence (the response to power and authority outside ourselves) to a condition of intra-dependence (the internalization of this power and authority within ourselves), unless for one reason or another we become stuck and the process breaks down.

Worship plays a key role in this oscillating process. Not only are we responding to what we experience externally, but there is internal movement as well. Our unconscious response to symbol and ritual can be for all of us an avenue of profound inner change, a change that we know far too little about and to which we pay far too little attention. The primary task of the Church, suggests the Grubb Institute's Bruce Reed, is to facilitate this oscillation process.

Such facilitation suggests to me not only the careful cultivation of a sense of mystery and awe, but also the cultivation of the kind of participation on the part of the congregation which produces a sense of mutuality and self-initiative. The movement in worship is from isolation to a sense of profound dependence, to the awareness that, within us, because of our union with Christ, we possess the power and authority we need to act on our own in His name. "The conscious, fully awakened act of performing the Liturgy," writes the noted Roman Catholic scholar von Hildebrand, "seals into the soul the Face of Christ. In taking part in the Liturgy, we make our own the fundamental attitudes embodied in it."[4] Though certainly mystical, it seems to me such an undertaking is fundamental to grasping the profound relationship which exists between our personal spiritual journeys and our participation in the worship of the Christian community. Each supports and shapes the other.

Christian worship is a ritual enactment of the movement of God in Christ, culminating in the various forms by which we commemorate the Lord's Supper. As Oscar Cullman has pointed out, the early Church understood itself to be united with the risen Christ in the closest possible way in the eucharistic celebration, which was regarded as the continuation of that first Easter meal on the road to Emmaus. Thus the Lord's presence was re-experienced during these love feasts, both as a recollection of the *historical* fact of the Resurrection and as an experience of the *contemporary* fact of His invisible coming in the gathering of Christians assembled to break bread.[5]

The experience of Christ, therefore, which takes place within us in the solitude of meditation is indissolubly connected with the liturgical experience of the Christian community. The telling of the story, the lifting up of word and song, the moments of silence, the prayers we offer on behalf of the human family, the breaking of bread—all of this is part of that process by which the transforming power of Christ does its work. It is the process which lies at the heart of God's healing and liberating activity in the world.

THE CONGREGATION
AS A SCHOOL FOR MINISTRY

How then might a congregation begin to develop a process for the calling forth and support of a ministry that is rooted in the life of prayer? The place to begin is in thanksgiving for what is already going on. In congregation after congregation, where there is no noticeable attempt to equip communicants for ministry, no formal system of support, the Spirit is nevertheless at work, sometimes despite us. Any attempt to strengthen the ministry of the congregation must of necessity begin here. Ministry *is* going on. There are people who have responded to the call of the Lord and have been chosen to share in His ministry, often in ways that are quiet and unnoticed. Concern for the development of the total ministry of the Church begins by identifying those already engaged in ministry and using their gifts for the calling forth of others. Wherever there is a community of Christians gathered for worship, the Spirit is at work. At best, all we ever do is to build on the fruit of that work so that what is begun may be deepened and sustained.

The congregation is by its very nature a school for ministry. Our task is to establish the kind of environment that allows the vision of what might be to deepen and enlarge while, simultaneously, building the structures by which this vision can be acted upon. Certainly one of the classic examples of how a group of people went about doing just this is the story of the Church of the Savior in Washington, D.C.[6] A group of people took Gordon Cosby's initial vision and moved with it. From the very beginning they were committed to both the inward journey from which ministry emerges and the outward journey where ministry is actually exercised. The structures they developed—disciplined mission groups which focused on particular areas of need—came out of their experience of worship, prayer and study. Structures were not imposed but, rather, were allowed to develop in response to the Spirit and in accord with the gifts which the members had been given.

The story of the Church of the Savior is an exciting one. It suggests *one* way in which *one* church has gone about developing its potential for ministry. But, like all models, it cannot be duplicated elsewhere. We can learn from what happened and is happening, but to impose what worked in *one* situation on another is to deny the very spirit which gave it birth. Each community must find its own way based on the particular gifts it possesses, while drawing what has been learned from others. There is no task any more exciting to which a congregation might devote its time and energy.

I have already suggested four educational elements that can be adapted and developed by the local church:

1. The nurturing of personal faith in the context of a Christian world view. (See particularly Chapter I.)

2. The development of covenant groups for the identification of gifts and the support of ministry. (See particularly Chapter II.)

3. Training in the disciplines of the Spirit. (See particularly Chapters III, IV and V.)

4. The training and support of special ministries, including the ministry of spiritual guidance. (See Chapter VI.)

I would like to take note of each of these elements, not so much to enlarge on what has already been said, but rather to suggest briefly some practical ways in which these elements might be built into a church program.

NURTURING PERSONAL FAITH

Personal faith is nurtured when, through the working of the Holy Spirit, our own personal stories interconnect at both a cognitive and effective level with the story of redemption. This involves opportunities for personal reflection and sharing, as well as the opportunity to explore the implications of *the* story for both oneself and the world.[7] In my own experience, the weekend conference is a major resource for this kind of faith development. Although it is often slow to catch on, once it is built into the ongoing program of the parish it becomes a major element in training for ministry.

St. Mark's Church in Mystic, Connecticut bases the major thrust of its ministry development program on what is called a "School of Christianity" which is run all year long. The school is structured around three types of groups, each with its own objectives. Fellowship Groups help persons deal with the issue of personal and corporate story on an informal basis. Study Groups offer the experience of Christian community which engages in the disciplined study of the Bible, worship, Church history and doctrine. Mission Groups (similar to what I have referred to as covenant groups) help members to think through the moral and ethical implications of their faith for their own lives. The Fellowship Groups meet monthly for six months with new groups being formed throughout the year. The Study Groups and Mission Groups meet weekly for six to eight weeks throughout the year, depending upon the particular objective involved. The Rev. Edward Adkins, the rector of this 400-member Episcopal Church, and his lay associate, Glennis Mollegen, are quick to point out that response to this rather intensive program was hardly immediate. It began with just a few people, but in four years has grown to include a major segment of the parish.

COVENANT GROUPS

Covenant Groups are the key to deepening one's sense of ministry. They are, as described earlier, gatherings of eight to twelve people who meet weekly or biweekly for mutual accountability and support. Within most congregations, ministries tend to focus on a particular cluster of concerns. There are ministries concerned primarily with "the building up of the Body": ministries of teaching, ministries of evangelism, ministries of caring, healing and administration, to name but a few. There are also ministries based in the parish but focused outward toward some community concern. There are ecumenical ministries that have their base outside the structures of the congregation. Any of these can provide the focus for covenants of accountability and support. They can also provide the encouragement that is needed for the development of the kind of personal discipline spoken about throughout this book. Many such covenant groups have developed common disciplines in which people not only pray for one another but where common lectionaries are developed so that individual meditation revolves around a common theme.

Groups of this kind are becoming more and more common throughout the Church. What has not been developed is a system of support for the many individual ministries that people exercise on their own within their jobs or in the community: ministries within offices, through volunteer agencies, in political campaigns, within neighborhoods where they live. These are the ministries which, because they are unorganized, generally go unnoticed and unaffirmed, although, in reality, they are the cutting edge of the Church's mission. As the sense of being called to ministry becomes normative in the life of a congregation, special attention needs to be given to the skills and information required to put our gifts to best use. The Church has a long history of training teachers for their ministry within the congregation but, all too often, this is as far as it goes. There is just as much need to train persons in pastoral skills, value clarification or evangelism, all ministries which require particular expertise. When such training also includes serious work in the disciplines of prayer, we will begin to see a new vision for the local church.

TRAINING IN PRAYER

The major ingredient in learning the disciplines of the spiritual life is to practice them. At the Hartford Seminary Foundation we have been working with congregations in three to six sessions, in a program which includes: Developing a Theology of Prayer, the Art of Meditation, and the Use of a Journal. This merely serves to get people started. In most cases the initial thrust has been picked up by the congregation with monthly gatherings and the use of spiritual companions. When these types of workshops are offered on a regular basis, in conjunction with the other elements of a ministry development program, prayer is seen not as something off by itself, but that which is necessary for the undergirding of ministry.

As pointed out earlier in this book, there is also a critical need for training in the ministry of spiritual guidance. There are persons within a congregation whose gifts make them particularly adept at this, largely because they take their own journey in Christ seriously and have the ability to help others. Such a training program would have to take place over a relatively long period of time in order to allow time for reading and for work with one's own discipline. It might include work in listening skills, the examination of some of the classics, the sharing of personal experiences in meditation, along with reflection on pertinent literature dealing with Christian theology and the discipline of spiritual direction. The key to such a program, however, would be the experience the participant had working with his or her own spiritual guide and serving under some supervisor as a guide to others.

FROM WANDERERS TO JOURNEYERS

No thoughtful person today needs to be convinced of the vast problems of the world in which we live. The gap between the haves and the have-nots is widening at breakneck speed as the resources available to us continue to shrink. As Christians we confront this world of ours, not as bystanders, but as people with a particular mission. We are a people called to share in the ministry of Jesus Christ. Our capacity to respond is directly related to the seriousness with which we approach the journey that is before us.

The rhythm of solitude and action is not an "extra" for Christians; it is the basis of our vocation. We are a people under obedience. The parish church serves as an instrument of God for the deepening of this sense of obedience. No task is of any greater importance in the world today. We are more than wanderers. We are engaged in a disciplined journey which leads to an ever-expanding awareness of Christ-in-us on behalf of the world.

Notes

INTRODUCTION

1. James C. Fenhagen, *Mutual Ministry* (New York: The Seabury Press, 1977), p. 96.

CHAPTER I

1. Elizabeth O'Connor, *The New Community* (New York: Harper & Row, 1976), pp. 57–58.
2. Robert A. Raines, *Living the Question* (Waco, Texas: Word, Inc., 1976), p. 32.
3. Loren Eiseley, *The Night Country* (New York: Scribner's, 1971), p. 224.
4. O'Connor, op. cit.
5. "Second Letter to the People of God," from *Sojourners* (May 1977), Vol. 6, no. 5, p. 20.

CHAPTER II

1. Nikos Kazantzakis, *Report to Greco* (New York: Simon & Schuster, 1965), p. 305.
2. William Swing, "From the Rector to You," St. Columba's Episcopal Church, 4201 Albemarle Street, N.W., Washington, D.C. 20016 (March 29, 1977).
3. John Sanford, *The Kingdom Within* (Philadelphia: J. B. Lippincott, 1970), pp. 173–74.
4. Urban T. Holmes, *Ministry and Imagination* (New York: The Seabury Press, 1976), p. 88.

5. Hans Küng, *On Being a Christian* (Garden City, N.Y.: Doubleday, 1976), p. 174.

CHAPTER III

1. Anthony Bloom, *Courage to Pray* (New York: Paulist Press, 1975), p. 5.
2. Martin Buber, *Between Man and Man* (New York: Macmillan, 1965), p. 14.
3. Thomas Merton, *New Seeds of Contemplation* (New York: New Directions, 1961), p. 37.
4. C. S. Lewis, *Poems* (New York: Harcourt, Brace and World, 1964), p. 122.
5. Henri Nouwen, *With Open Hands* (Notre Dame, Indiana: Ave Maria Press, 1972), p. 12.

CHAPTER IV

1. William Johnston, *The Still Point* (New York: Harper & Row, 1971), p. 151.
2. Avery Brooke, *How to Meditate Without Leaving the World* (Norton, Connecticut: Vineyard Books, 1975).
3. Thomas Merton, *New Seeds of Contemplation* (New York: New Directions, 1961), p. 3.
4. Morton Kelsey, *The Other Side of Silence* (New York: Paulist Press, 1976), p. 8.
5. St. Teresa of Avila, *Interior Castle*, E. Alliston Peers, tr. (Garden City, N.Y.: Doubleday/Image, 1961), p. 231.
6. *The Cloud of Unknowing*, Ira Progoff, tr. (New York: Dell/Delta, 1957), pp. 224–25.

CHAPTER V

1. Lewis Carroll, *Alice in Wonderland*, Vol. 5 (New York: Collier/New Junior Classics, 1938), p. 51.
2. Jacques Ellul, *Prayer and Modern Man* (New York: The Seabury Press, 1973), p. 116.

3. "Kirkridge Readings and Intentions, 1976," Kirkridge, Bangor, Pennsylvania 18013.

4. Henri Nouwen, *Reaching Out* (Garden City, N.Y.: Doubleday, 1975), p. 96.

5. Morton Kelsey, *The Other Side of Silence* (New York: Paulist Press, 1976).

6. Ira Progoff, *The Symbolic and the Real* (New York: McGraw Hill, 1963), pp. 74, 76. For a more extensive development of the use of the journal by Dr. Progoff, see also *At a Journal Workshop* (New York: Dialogue House Library, 1975).

7. Dag Hammarskjold, *Markings* (New York: Alfred A. Knopf, 1964), p. 411.

8. Ibid., p. 154.

9. Morton Kelsey, *God, Dreams, and Revelation* (Minneapolis: Augsburg, 1974), p. 201.

10. Raymond Blakney, *Meister Eckhardt* (New York: Harper & Row, 1941), p. 9.

CHAPTER VI

1. John H. Wright, "A Discussion of Spiritual Direction," *Studies in the Spirituality of the Jesuits* (March 1972), Vol. LV, No. 2.

2. William Connolly, "Appealing to Strength in Spiritual Direction," *Review for Religions* (September 1973), Vol. 32, No. 5.

3. Dag Hammarskjold, *Markings* (New York: Alfred A. Knopf, 1964), p. 122.

4. Elizabeth O'Connor, *Journey Inward, Journey Outward* (New York: Harper & Row, 1968);

_____, *Our Many Selves* (New York: Harper & Row, 1971);

_____, *Search for Silence* (Waco, Texas: Word, Inc., 1974);

_____, *The New Community* (New York: Harper & Row, 1976).

Henri Nouwen, *With Open Hands* (Notre Dame, Indiana: Ave Maria Press, 1972);

_____, *Out of Solitude* (Notre Dame, Indiana: Ave Maria Press, 1976);

———, *The Wounded Healer* (Garden City, N.Y.: Doubleday, 1972);

———, *Reaching Out* (Garden City, N.Y.: Doubleday, 1975);

———, *Genesee Diary* (Garden City, N.Y.: Doubleday, 1976).

5. Raymond Blakney, *Meister Eckhardt* (New York: Harper & Row, 1941), p. 51.

6. Ibid., p. 23.

7. The spiritual classics referred to have all been published many times, in a variety of editions. Listed below are the titles and publishers of the editions I have had access to:

Helen Waddell, *The Desert Fathers* (Ann Arbor, Michigan: University of Michigan Press, 1957);

St. Teresa of Avila, *Interior Castle*, E. Allison Peers, tr. (Garden City, N.Y.: Doubleday/Image, 1961);

Raymond Blakney, *Meister Eckhardt* (New York: Harper & Row, 1941);

Francis de Sales, *Introduction to a Devout Life* (Cleveland, Ohio: World, 1952);

The Cloud of Unknowing, Ira Progoff, tr. (New York: Dell/Delta, 1957);

The Way of the Pilgrim, R. M. French, tr. (New York: Harper & Row, 1952);

Igumen Chariton, *The Art of Prayer* (London: Faber & Faber, 1966).

CHAPTER VII

1. *The Way of the Pilgrim*, R. M. French, tr. (New York: Harper & Row, 1952), p. 1.

2. Timothy Ware in his introduction to *The Art of Prayer*, an Orthodox anthology compiled by Igumen Chariton (London: Faber & Faber, 1966), p. 28.

3. Bruce Reed, "The Task of the Church and the Role of its Members," an Alban Institute Publication, Mt. St. Alban, Washington, D.C., 1975.

4. Dietrich von Hildebrand, *Liturgy and Personality* (New York: Longmans, Green, 1943), p. 19.

5. Oscar Cullman, "The Meaning of the Lord's Supper in Primitive Christianity," *Ecumenical Studies in Worship*, No. 1 (London: Lutterworth Press, 1958), p. 13.

6. The development of the Church of the Savior has been described by Elizabeth O'Connor in a number of books. For further exploration I would suggest *Call to Commitment; Journey Inward, Journey Outward;* and *The New Community,* all published by Harper & Row. Also, Gordon Cosby's *Handbook for Mission Groups* (Waco, Texas: Word, Inc., 1975).

7. For further discussion on the use of "story" in faith development, see the chapter on storytelling in my book *Mutual Ministry* (New York: The Seabury Press, 1977).